GCSE PASS

GEOGRAPHY

Vivien Perry

First published 1988
by Charles Letts & Co Ltd
Diary House, Borough Road, London SE1 1DW

Illustrations: Peter McClure

British Library Cataloguing in Publication Data

Perrry, Vivien C.
  Geography . – (Key facts. GCSE passbooks).
  1. Geography – Textbooks – 1945-
  I. Title II. Series
  910   G128
ISBN 0 85097 806 8

Acknowledgements

I should like to express my gratitude to Norman Law for checking the manuscript at each stage and for all the invaluable suggestions he made for improving the style and content of this book.

Vivien Perry, 1988

Contents

	Page
Preface	6
Introduction and guide to using this book	7
Introduction to GCSE Geography	8
Hints on how to approach Geography examinations	10
A sample revision programme	12
1 Diagrams and maps	14
2 Ordnance Survey maps	24
3 The nature of the earth	29
4 Shaping the landscape	36
5 Understanding weather and climate	52
6 Population	59
7 Where people live	79
8 Farming	94
9 Resources for industry	108
10 Manufacturing industry	121
11 Services	133
12 Development and trade	142
Answers to questions	153
Final examination advice	160

The introduction of GCSE Geography has helped students, because the different syllabuses emphasize the importance of understanding the environment in which we live. Geography no longer depends on learning information that bears little relation to everyday life. Instead, studies are aimed at giving insights into the way we live, and how we relate to different environments.

Testing the level you have reached in your studies no longer depends only on examination performance. The results of continuous assessment are a major part of your final grade. Coursework, field studies and projects all contribute to that final grade. For some of you, coursework comprises 50 per cent of your total possible marks. However well you may do in your examination, it cannot make up for low marks in coursework.

This book is designed to help you with the examination part of your course, to add to those marks you have already gained in the past months. While it cannot make up for poor work in the past, careful use of this book can contribute to a better examination performance. This should help you avoid some of the common examination pitfalls, and therefore achieve a higher final grade.

The exam aims to test you in several ways:

1 In skills.
2 In knowledge and understanding.
3 In values and attitudes.

During your course you should have mastered a number of skills. Class exercises will have given you plenty of experience in handling material in a number of ways. You should also have absorbed a lot of knowledge, giving you some understanding of the interactions in the environment. Many of the issues you have studied are open to different views. By now you should have some opinions about matters like pollution, conservation, inner cities, unemployment and development. You should also be able to appreciate how other people may have differing opinions that are equally valid.

This book can help you prepare for the exam, but it cannot supply all the background you have obtained through your coursework. Most of the contents are related to knowledge and understanding. The book provides a summary of the main areas and subjects about which you require information. Key concepts and skills are explained. It is not necessary to learn the entire contents.

First of all you should study chapters 1 and 2. These will remind you of the various methods you have already learnt and will give you some more practice in handling data. Before you commence working through the other chapters, study the table on page 9. Different exam syllabuses cover different topics. You do not need to revise topics that are not in your syllabus. Find out the name of your syllabus, then mark off all those parts of this book which relate to that syllabus.

Finally, a word about case studies. You will have studied many examples from Britain and the rest of the world. It is **your** examples that you need to revise. The case studies in this book include many of the most common ones. When they are the same as yours, use them to help your revision. If they are different, read them to broaden your knowledge of the topic but revise your own case studies.

K ▶ Throughout the book, important points to which you should pay particular attention are denoted by the special '**K**' symbol.

The following details will help to give you a more general idea of the background thinking to your syllabus. Read through the criteria so that you will know which aspects of your course to concentrate on.

The National Criteria for Geography

Aims

Knowledge and understanding
1 To develop a sense of place and an understanding of relative location.
2 To develop an awareness of the characteristics and distribution of a number of contrasting physical and human environments.
3 To develop an understanding of some of the processes which affect the development of environments.
4 To promote an understanding of the spatial effects of the ways in which people interact with each other and with their environments.
5 To encourage an understanding of different communities and cultures within our society and elsewhere in the world, together with an awareness of people's active role in interacting with environments.

Skills
To develop a range of skills through practical work, including investigations in the field, associated with observation, collection, representation, analysis, interpretation and use of data, including maps and photographs.

Values
1 To develop a sensitive awareness of the environment.
2 To encourage you to appreciate the significance of the attitudes and values of those who make decisions about the management of the environment and the use of terrestial space.
3 To make you aware of the contrasting opportunities and constraints facing people living in different places under different physical and human conditions.

Content guidelines

The following elements of content are essential:
1 A first-hand study of a small area, preferably the student's home area.
2 A study of contrasting areas and/or themes within the British Isles. All studies should include such aspects of geography as the physical environment, population, settlements, agriculture, extractive, processing and manufacturing industries, tertiary activities and communications.

3 A consideration of the United Kingdom's relationships, for
example in trade and industry, with wider groupings of nations, such
as the EEC.
4 A study of the geographical aspects of important social and
environmental issues. These include the problems and opportunities
of development in less affluent nations, the problems of large cities,
the control and management of resources, and the human response to
hostile or hazardous environments.
5 Topics which focus your attention on the interrelationship and
interaction between peoples and their environments.

Chapters 1, 2, 6, 7, 8, 9, 10, 11 and 12 need to be studied for every
syllabus. The following table indicates which sections of the book can
be omitted for different syllabuses.

Examination Board	Syllabus	Section to be omitted
London and East Anglia	A, B	Chapter 3
Midland	C	Inside the earth
Northern	A, B, C	Faulting
Southern	B	
Welsh Joint		
Scotland		
London and East Anglia	A, B	Chapter 4
Midland	A, C	Glaciation
Northern	A, B, C	
Southern	B	
Midland	C	Chapter 5
Northern	A, B, C	Heat, pressure and wind,
Southern	B	weather patterns, weather
		maps, factors affecting climate
London and East Anglia	B	Chapter 11
Midland	C	Transport
Northern	A, D	
Southern	A, B	
Welsh Joint		
Scotland		
Midland	A, B	Chapter 12
Northern	A	Trade
Welsh Joint		

Hints on how to approach Geography examinations

What you need for the exam

For a Geography exam it is vital to have a good ruler marked off in centimetres and millimetres. Several hard lead pencils, well-sharpened, are useful. It is better to complete maps and diagrams in pencil than in ball-point because the finished work is neater and mistakes can be erased. For that reason a pencil eraser is useful as well. You can use coloured pencils in an exam to highlight points on maps and diagrams, but they are not essential. If you have them, resist the temptation of spending a lot of time during the exam colouring in maps. Geometry instruments are not vital, but dividers provide a quick way of measuring distance on maps, and protractors for measuring percentages on pie charts, so if you have them, take them.

It is acceptable to write in ball-point pen, but make sure you have a spare one. If you use an ink pen, check that you have a spare cartridge or that you have filled your pen immediately before the exam.

Selecting the questions

First of all, check how many questions you are supposed to answer. Make sure you answer questions from the correct number of sections. Read the questions carefully. It is very important to make sure that you have understood the question correctly. Particularly in multiple-choice questions which are done quickly, it is easy to misread questions and therefore give the wrong answer.

When you have a choice of questions, do not choose the question that seems simplest but choose the one you know most about. It is important to check the number of marks for each part of a question. Often the easiest parts carry only a few marks. So make sure you choose questions where you can answer the parts that carry the most marks, even if you cannot answer all the short parts. Remember that many of the answers to the short parts can be found in the maps, diagrams and photographs accompanying the question. Study these carefully and extract the information. Do not try to guess the answers.

To make sure that you answer the questions correctly, you can mark the key words and phrases. Once you have chosen the question, read it through again. Draw a box around words that tell you what to do (direction words, e.g. describe, explain, state, comment on, etc.) Then underline the subject of the question, e.g. pattern of settlement, location of industry, physical features, etc. Finally, circle the area or example to which the question refers, e.g. a traditional industrial region, a new town, a city in the developing world, northern England, etc. By doing this, you will be able to see at a glance the main elements of the question without getting confused by all the other information in the question.

Plan your time carefully. Do not spend too long on drawing. Make sure you allow enough time to answer the high-mark sections. If you run very short of time towards the end, concentrate on the high-mark sections of your final question. Try to leave time at the end for checking through your answers.

Do not leave learning your work until just before an exam. The aim of revision is to remind you of what you have already studied and understood. Try to keep a regular pattern of studying and checking your work throughout the two years of your course.

This revision programme is based on:

1 The assumption that you have already done class tests from time to time.

2 The fact that you have already revised for previous exams during your course.

You need to commence your revision programme at Easter. Divide your available time per week by the number of subjects you have to revise. Make sure that you revise Geography at least once a week while you are still having lessons. It is worth remembering that revising **little and often** will ensure that you remember things better when it comes to the actual examination.

1 Work through Chapter 1.
Check back to your course book for anything which you are unsure about.

2 Work though Chapter 2.
Revise the Ordnance Survey symbols from your course book.

3 Make two lists. One should be a list of the case studies you have done: check which of them are included in this book, and mark the ones you need to revise from your course books. For the second list, write down the sections and case studies you need to revise from this book.

4 Read through a chapter at a time. Attempt the sample questions at the end of the chapter and check the answers. Go back to the mistakes and work out where you went wrong. Then go on to the next chapter.

5 Learn the case studies.

6 The day before the exam, go over the key words related to the subjects which are likely to be on the paper.

Revision is a personal matter, and no two people work in exactly the same way. One method has just been described. If that does not suit your way of working, there are other methods you can attempt. One is to use your cassette recorder. As you work through the book, read out what you think are the most important points you need to remember, and record what you have read. Then play back your tape from time to time. If your cassette recorder is portable and has earphones, you can listen to the tapes as you walk to school or wait for the bus. Replaying a section of tape each night before you go to bed can also help you. Check the next morning to see how much you remember from the tape played the night before. You might be surprised to discover you can remember most of it!

Another method which you might find helpful involves making up a series of cards. Buy a set of index cards from your local stationer. On each card write at the top the subject, e.g. river action, types of farming, etc. On the left-hand side of the card, write down the key words for that topic, and then write a brief explanation or description beside it. You can buy a set of *Geography Passcards* to accompany this book, which will help your last-minute revision. However, making your own as well can help, because as you look up the words and write them down they become clearer and you are more likely to remember them. Also, you can produce cards for the topics on your course that may not be included in this book.

Remember you cannot leave revision until the night before. All you can hope to do at that stage is to refresh your memory on the key points. You may have two exams on the same day. If you do, divide your time to allow last minute revision for both.

1 Diagrams and maps

Aims of this chapter

By the end of this chapter you should be able to:

1 Find out information from diagrams and maps.
2 Plot values on line and bar graphs.
3 Describe features shown in photographs.

Information in diagrams

Maps and diagrams occur in most exam questions to test your graphic skills and to help you answer the questions. Many questions ask you to extract information and then to interpret it. Some also ask you to plot values on to frames.

Line graphs

These are used to show changes over a period of time.

Simple line graphs are composed of a base line to show time and a vertical scale for the values. The values for each point in time are plotted against the vertical scale and joined together by a line.

Figure 1 shows population growth. To find the total for a year, place your ruler vertically against the year. For the point at which the line and ruler meet, read the vertical scale. To find the year in which a named value was reached, place your ruler horizontally from the vertical scale, then read the year from the base line.

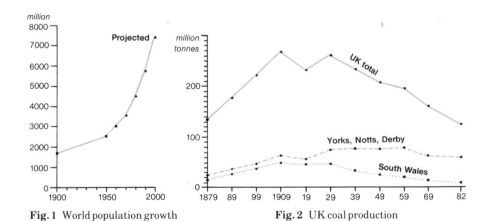

Fig. 1 World population growth

Fig. 2 UK coal production

A compound line graph is constructed in the same way, but several sets of values are plotted. Different types of lines or labelling are used for each set of values. Figure 2 shows UK coal production between 1879 and 1982.

Bar graphs

The values are marked off on a vertical scale. Columns of equal width are drawn to a height parallel to their values on the vertical scale. Bar graphs are commonly used to show information when only one value is numerical. To find out the output of a country in fig. 3, read off the value from the vertical scale level with the top of the column.

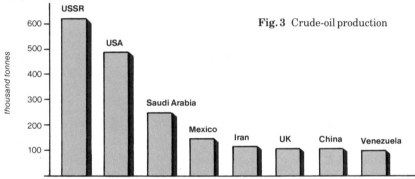

Fig. 3 Crude-oil production

Divided rectangle

This is a bar divided into parts proportional to the value of each part. Sometimes the bar represents 100 per cent, and each segment is a percentage of the total. When actual figures are used, the length of the bar is proportional to the total. Several rectangles may be constructed on the same scale, so that comparisons can be made. Figure 4 shows the death tolls from natural disasters. Work out the total of any part by subtracting the lower from the higher value along the scale.

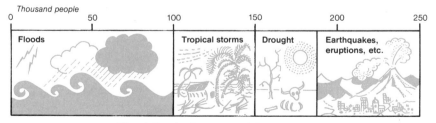

Fig. 4 Deaths from natural disasters, per year

Pie charts

These are like divided rectangles, but with a circle representing the total amount. When more than one pie chart is used, the size of each circle is proportional to the total amount. Each quarter of the circle is equal to 25 per cent of the circle's value.

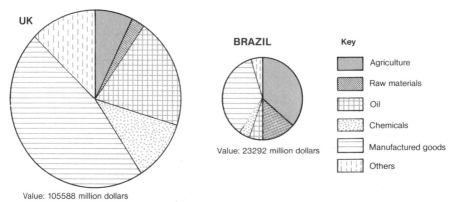

Fig. 5 Main exports of the UK and Brazil

Triangular graphs

Each side of the triangle represents one category of the total. A dot or cross is marked at the place where the three values meet. To read off

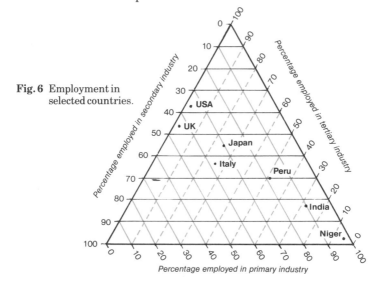

Fig. 6 Employment in selected countries.

the values of a point, follow the nearest lines to where they meet the outer frame.

Information on maps

Located bar graphs and pie charts
Sometimes line graphs, bar graphs, divided rectangles or pie graphs are located on maps. In this way, information is given about values in a geographical context.

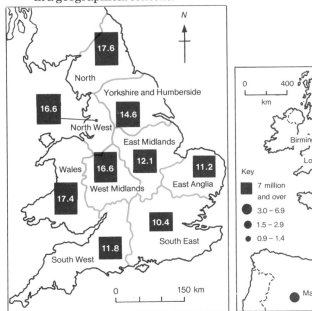

Fig. 7 Unemployment in England and Wales

Fig. 8 Major cities of the European Economic Community

Dot maps
Distribution is often shown on a map by dots. Dots represent a certain number, e.g. one dot may equal 1000 people. The dots are located, as far as possible, where the people are. Sometimes the size of the dot or circle is proportional to the total, as shown in fig. 8.

Isoline maps
An isoline joins together places with an equal value. Isolines include: contours, joining places of equal height; isobars, which join places of equal atmospheric pressure; and isotherms, which join together places of equal temperature.

To interpret an isoline map, you need to identify patterns. Areas of lowest and highest values can be recognized. The closer together isolines are, the greater the change that is occurring over an area, e.g. when contours are very close together, it means that the slope of the land is steep.

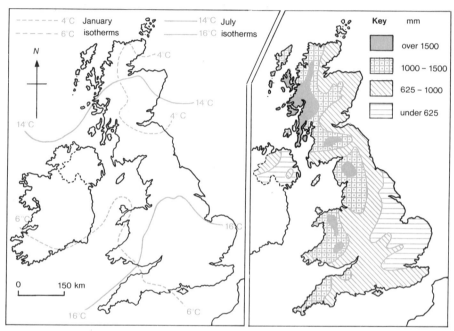

Fig. 9 UK temperatures   **Fig. 10** UK rainfall

Density shading
Often the regions created by isolines are shaded, like in fig. 10. This is called density shading, which changes from very light for low densities or numbers to very dark for high densities. It is also used for regions or countries to show density values, e.g. people per sq. km., percentage of arable land, etc.

Flow charts
These show movement, often of people or traffic. A line is drawn along the route taken, proportional in width to the number of people or amount of traffic. Therefore the thickest line shows the greatest volume. You find out the actual number by measuring the width of the line against the scale.

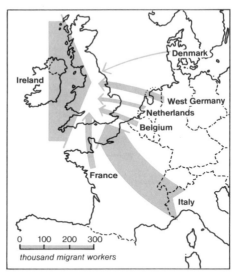

Fig. 11 European migrant workers in the UK

Sketches and sketch maps

Drawing sketch maps

Some questions provide a frame in which you are asked to draw a map or plan of an area you have studied. Try to learn the main features of the maps you have used in your coursework as examples of topics. Memorize the shapes of the maps and the location and names of the principal towns, physical features, regions and economic activities. Practise drawing them, and attempt to do them quickly. In the examination, draw the features clearly and label them. Do not waste time by block shading, it is quicker to use line shading. Do not forget a direction arrow and a scale when these are needed.

More often, you are asked to draw or complete sketches. These are easier to learn and quicker to draw. Only include the main features. As with sketch maps, careful labelling is most important.

Using sketch maps

You can obtain a lot of information from maps which are supplied with questions. First of all, check exactly what the map shows, then its scale and key. Do not overlook any of the symbols. Each one is given for a reason. Using the scale, you can work out distances

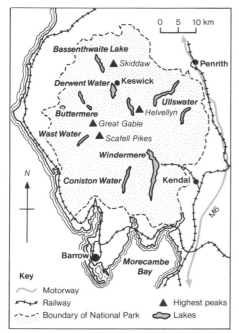

Fig. 12 The Lake District National Park

between different places or symbols. Measure the distance on the map, then convert it to actual distance by multiplying by the scale. The location of symbols helps you work out the relationships between different features on the map.

Landscape sketches and block diagrams
Interpret these in a similar way to maps, as in fig. 13.

Block diagrams also give you structural information, so that you can relate the surface features to what is underneath.

Photographs

Many questions include photographs. Some are provided simply for recognition of features such as terraced housing or a modern factory. Others need to be analysed, e.g. aerial photographs with a view of a landscape or industry. As with sketch maps, it is important to identify features correctly.

Questions might be about the field pattern, the position or type of settlement, the physical features, the type of industry. Remember that evidence to support a statement must come from the photograph; you do not need to guess at an answer. Only give the information asked for.

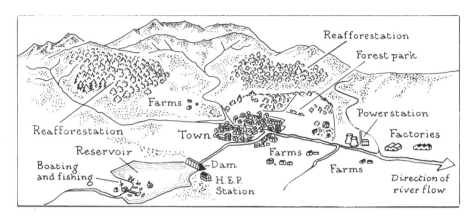

Fig. 13 Economic uses of a river basin

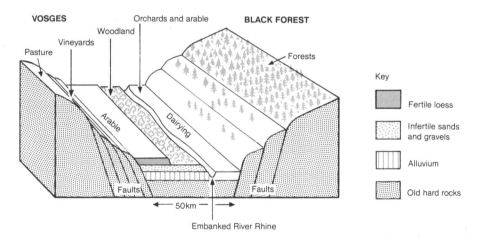

Fig. 14 Land use in the Rhine Rift Valley

Other sources of information

Information is often presented in other ways. You may be asked to discuss cartoons or advertisements which make a particular point. Extracts from newspapers or from books should be read very carefully.

Summary

1 Information is given in questions through diagrams, maps or photographs.
2 These can be analysed and interpreted.
3 Construction of line or bar graphs may be required.

Questions

1 Look at fig. 1 on page 14.
(a) In what year did world population reach three billion?
(b) By how much did world population grow between 1960 and 1980?
2 Look at fig. 2 on page 14.
(a) Which coalfield had the highest output of coal in the year that British production reached its peak?
(b) From what coalfield has production declined the most since 1929?
3 Look at fig. 3 on page 15.
(a) Which country has the highest production?
(b) What was the total production of the three countries with the highest output?
4 Look at fig. 4 on page 15.
(a) Which type of disaster causes the most deaths?
(b) What proportion of deaths are caused by disasters related to climate?
5 Look at fig. 5 on page 16.
(a) Which country exports the greater value of foodstuffs?
(b) What percentage of the UK's exports are manufactured goods?
6 Look at fig. 6 on page 16.
(a) What percentage of the workforce of Peru is in primary employment?
(b) Which country has the highest percentage in tertiary employment?
7 Look at fig. 7 on page 17.
(a) Which region has the highest unemployment rate?
(b) The national average for unemployment is 11.1 per cent. Name one region with below average unemployment.
8 Look at fig. 8 on page 17.
(a) Name the largest city in the EEC.

(b) Which country has the greatest number of cities with between 0.9 and 2.9 million people?

9 Look at fig. 9 on page 18.

(a) What is the highest average summer temperature?

(b) What region of the UK is coldest in summer and winter?

10 Look at fig. 10 on page 18.

(a) What is the lowest annual rainfall in the UK?

(b) What do the regions of highest rainfall have in common?

11 Look at fig. 11 on page 19.

(a) How many workers come from Italy?

(b) Which country supplies the greatest number of migrant workers?

12 Look at fig. 12 on page 20.

(a) List three activities for tourists.

(b) What natural attractions are found there?

13 Look at fig. 13 on page 21.

(a) Give three examples of different economic land uses in river basins.

(b) Describe the location of one such land use.

14 Look at fig. 14 on page 21.

(a) What are the lowest terraces used for?

(b) Of what rock are the Horst mountains made?

2 Ordnance Survey maps

Aims of this chapter

After working through this chapter you should be able to:

1 Identify features on Ordnance Survey (OS) maps.
2 Work out grid references, direction, distance and gradients.
3 Draw cross-sections and sketch maps.
4 Interpret features on OS maps and photographs.
   OS questions require the use of a number of skills. Without these it
is not possible to interpret map information.

Working with OS maps

Recognizing symbols
You need to be able to recognize all symbols used on an OS map. Look
back to your coursework where you have them listed. The best way of
memorizing symbols is to divide them into groups:

1 Physical features, e.g. cliffs, exposed rocks.
2 Vegetation, e.g. woodland, marsh, etc.
3 Settlement, e.g. churches, street patterns.
4 Communications, e.g. class of road or railway.

Direction
When you are asked to state a direction, start from the point 'from'
and follow the direction to the point 'to'. Learn the sixteen points of
the compass. Grid north is always at the top of the map.

Grid references
Grid references identify locations precisely. You will need to find
locations from grid references given in questions, and work out your
own grid references for features when asked.
   A four-figure grid reference is given to identify a grid square. The
reference is that of the bottom left-hand (south-west) corner of the
square. The first two figures represent the vertical line (called an
easting, because the vertical lines are numbered from west to east),
and the second two figures represent the horizontal line (called a
northing, because the horizontal lines are numbered from south to
north).

With six-figure references, the first two numbers represent the vertical line and the fourth and fifth numbers represent the horizontal line. The third and sixth numbers refer to the number of tenths of the square beyond the two lines. You have to estimate the number of tenths, because they are not marked on the map.

Distance and scale
A straight-line distance is measured with a ruler and then converted using the scale. Winding distances, like along a road or river, can be measured with a piece of paper or a pair of dividers. Mark the beginning on the edge of the paper, mark a point at each turn or bend and reorientate the paper. When using dividers, set them to a short space, perhaps 1 cm. and then 'walk' them along, turning at each point, adding up the number of turns. To convert the distances you have measured to the actual distance, you can put the piece of paper or ruler against the linear scale and read it off. Alternatively, you can calculate according to the representative fraction shown on the map.

You are likely to be given an OS extract at the scale of 1:50 000 or 1:25 000. Measure in centimetres, so that the calculation is simpler. Multiply the number of centimetres by the fraction (i.e. by 50 000 or 25 000). Then divide by 100 for the number of metres, or by 100 000 for the number of kilometres. The same method is followed, whatever the scale of the map. However, it is simplest just to remember that 1 cm. equals 0.5 km. on the 1:50 000 map, and 0.25 km. on the 1:25 000 map.

Gradients
The gradient is the steepness of a slope. To work out the gradient of a slope, mark the points at each end, usually given by grid reference. Find the height of each of these points, from the nearest contour or spot height. Subtract one from the other. That will give you the height difference in metres. Next, measure the distance between the two points and convert that into metres (i.e. the number of centimetres measured, multiplied by the representative fraction and divided by a hundred). The gradient is the distance divided by the height:

Distance between the two points
Height difference between the two points

This is written as '1 in [distance divided by height]'. Gradients of 1 in 5 or less are very steep, and between 1 in 5 and 1 in 7 are steep. Gradients over 1 in 30 are gentle.

Cross-sections

You may be asked to draw a cross-section. The frame for the cross-section is usually provided on the examination paper. Alternatively, you may be given a completed cross-section to relate to the OS map. To draw a cross-section:

1 Put the edge of a piece of paper along the line between two points specified in the question, and mark each end and every point at which a contour meets that piece of paper. Then note the heights of the contours onto your piece of paper.

2 Lay the edge of the piece of paper along the base line. Ensure that the points at each end correspond to those on the frame. At each place on the paper where there is a contour, mark the point on the frame at the height of the contour. Then join up the points.

A sketch cross-section can be done more quickly. Only the main contours are marked off.

Cross-sections may appear in other questions. Usually they involve some aspect of physical geography, like a river valley.

Sketch maps

These may occur in questions in two ways. One involves adding information from the OS map to the sketch map; the other requires drawing a sketch map on a frame provided. Use grid lines to help you locate contours, rivers or other features in the frame. Check that you are drawing the area asked for. Put in only the features asked for. Do not spend too much time shading.

Understanding OS maps

Most questions ask for interpretation of map evidence. First of all, find map evidence and then use your geographical knowledge to explain it.

Physical features

These are recognized by symbols or by contour patterns. Height is found from contours and from spot heights. Steepness of slope is judged by the intervals between contours; the closer the contours, the steeper the slope. Sometimes it is possible to identify rock type, e.g. an area without streams or rivers but with springs at a lower height often indicates that the rock is chalk or limestone.

Economic activities

Most evidence of economic activities comes from names on the map, e.g. farm names, factory, mine, etc. or symbols, e.g. quarry, government building. Recreation or tourism may be identified by features like a golf course, hotel or reservoir.

Settlement
'Settlement' may refer to a building, a village, a town or section of an urban area. The pattern of settlement is its distribution in the given area: dense, sparse, scattered, dispersed, nucleated, built-up, etc. Site is the land on which the settlement stands, e.g. valley, slope, riverside, bridging point, etc. Situation is its location related to other places, hills, rivers, towns, communications. Layout is the pattern of buildings in a settlement.

Communications
Roads, motorway, rail, airport, docks, ferries. There are four aspects: direction, links, routes, and associated features, e.g. stations. Often questions on routes are linked to physical features or settlements.

Using photographs with OS maps

A photograph of part of the area shown on the OS map may be included. Some questions may be based on evidence from the photograph alone, but often the two need to be referred to together. The name of a river on the photograph is found by working out how it is orientated to the map, and extracting the name from the map. Orientating is accomplished by relating features on the photograph to symbols and patterns on the map.

Summary

1 OS maps can be analysed with the help of techniques like symbol recognition, and use of grid references.

2 Direction, distance and gradient can be worked out from an OS map.

3 Cross-sections and sketch maps can be drawn of parts of OS maps.

4 From map evidence it is possible to learn quite a lot about the physical and human geography of the area shown.

5 Photographs can be used in relation to OS maps.

Questions

Using the OS map extract inside the back cover of this book, scale 1:25 000, answer the following questions:

1 What do the symbols mean at grid references 171534 and 181508?

2 Give the six-figure grid reference for the sewage works at Pixham.
3 In what direction is Juniper Hall (173527) from Mickleham Hall (170533)?
4 What is the distance by rail in km. from Dorking North Station (171504) to Westhumble Station (167519)?
5 Give three pieces of map evidence for early settlement in the area.
6 The hills east of the River Mole are composed of chalk.
(a) Find two pieces of map evidence to support this statement.
(b) What indication is there on the map that this area is used for recreation?
7 List three differences between the settlement patterns of Mickleham and Westhumble.
8 Draw a sketch cross-section of the Mole Valley between 160513 and 175513. Label the river, the flood plain, and the scarp slope.
9 (a) Draw a sketch map of the area shown by the map.
Divide the map into two regions, the valley and the Downs, and label those regions. Mark on to the map the main roads and railway lines.
(b) How has relief affected the pattern of communications?

Aims of this chapter

By the end of this chapter you should know about:

1 The structure of the earth.
2 The formation of mountains.
3 How different rocks have formed, and the landscapes they produce.

Inside the earth

The earth is made up of different layers, as fig. 1 shows. Many features of the earth's surface are due to variations in the crust. The main division is between continents and oceans. Continents are composed of **shields**, e.g. the Canadian shield, the Baltic shield, made of very ancient, hard rocks that are covered by a layer of sedimentary rocks. On the edges of the shields are fold mountains.

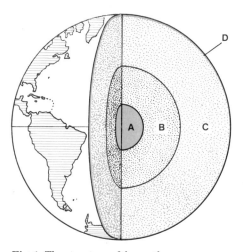

Key

A Inner core of very
      heavy substances
      1200 km thickness

B Outer core of liquid metals
      2200 km thickness

C Mantle of rocks
      2900 km thickness

D Crust, made mainly of granite
      and basalt
      8–40 km thickness

Fig. 1 The structure of the earth

The crust of the earth is made up of **plates** of solid rock floating on the plastic material of the upper mantle. The forces that cause changes in the earth's structure are called **tectonics**. Therefore, the activities associated with the plates are known as **plate tectonics**. The plates are enormous, often several thousand kilometres across, and between about 70 km. deep under the oceans and 150 km. deep under the continents. The plates were created by molten rock (magma) welling up from the depths of the earth along lines of weakness, and then spreading outwards.

As fig. 2 shows, some plates are moving towards one another (convergence), and away from others (divergence). Along the plate boundaries, earthquakes and volcanic eruptions occur.

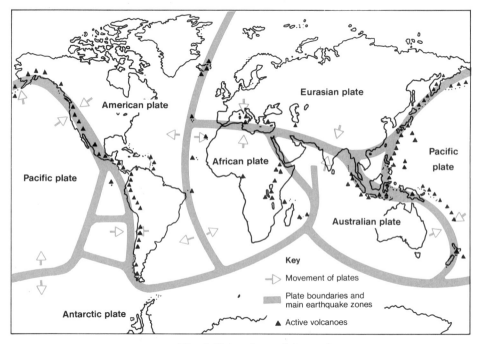

Fig. 2 Major plates of the earth

Mountain building is associated with the movement of plates. As plates converge, the sedimentary layers above buckle upwards to form fold mountains. The highest mountain ranges of the world were formed during the Alpine **orogeny** (orogeny = mountain building period). They are the highest because they are the most recently formed and have been worn down less than older mountain ranges. Alpine ranges include the Andes, South America; the Western Cordillera, North America; the Himalayas, Asia; and the European Alps.

Faulting

Sometimes forces from the mantle cause rock to crack or fracture along lines of weakness. If the rocks on either side of the fracture move, the crack is called a **fault**. Figure 3 shows a normal fault, where one block slides down relative to the other. If there are parallel faults, the land between them may sink, so forming a **rift valley**, or rise to form a **horst**. In West Germany, both are found.

Fig. 3 Faulting

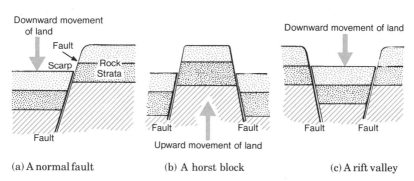

(a) A normal fault   (b) A horst block   (c) A rift valley

Groundwater

Water stored in rocks is called groundwater. The **water table** is the level below which the rock is saturated. The level of water table varies according to the amount of water soaking into the rock from the surface, and is higher after periods of heavy rain. If the water table reaches the surface, water will lie on the surface.

    Pervious rocks like limestone and chalk allow water to pass through them. Chalk allows water to pass through because it is porous, having tiny pores through which water seeps. Limestone is not porous, but as it formed it developed bedding planes and joints through which water may pass. Rocks that do not allow water to pass through are called **impervious**.

Types of rock

Rocks form in three main ways. **Igneous** rocks are formed from molten material (magma) welling up from the mantle. **Sedimentary** rocks are formed from sediments that have been worn away from existing rocks and compressed into layers of rock. **Metamorphic** rocks were originally igneous or sedimentary rocks, that have been changed by great heat or pressure.

Type	Appearance	Formation	Example
Igneous			
Granite	Hard, acid, crystalline	Igneous intrusion	Dartmoor
Basalt	Fine, dark, basic	Igneous extrusion	Antrim Plateau
Sedimentary			
Sandstone	Crystalline, acid	Layers of cemented sand	Exmoor
Coal:			
lignite	Brown coal	In Carboniferous	Coalfields
bituminous	Household coal.	times, swamp and	of UK, see
anthracite	Very hard, black coal	forest vegetation decayed to form peat, then was compressed	fig. 3, Ch. 9
Clay:	Fine particles of mud or silt, soft, impervious		
alluvium		Deposited by rivers	London Basin
boulder clay		Deposited by ice sheets and glaciers	East Anglia
Chalk	Soft, porous, composed of calcium carbonate	Remains of marine animals collected on floors of still seas, then compressed	Chilterns, North and South Downs
Limestone	Like chalk but harder. Pervious – water passes through joints	Similar to chalk. Often silt mixed in with calcium	Hard, Carb-oniferous: Pennines. Softer, Jurassic: Cotswolds
Metamorphic			
Slate	Thin beds, black, brittle	Metamorphosed shales	N. Wales
Gneisses and schists	Acid, hard crystalline	Metamorphosed granites	Scottish Highlands
Marble	Hard, shiny, veined	Metamorphosed limestone	Connemara, W. Ireland

Fig. 4 Rocks and their formation

Granite scenery, e.g. Dartmoor

Dartmoor is dome shaped, reaching a highest point of 622 metres. Above the rounded outline of the landscape are rock masses called **tors**. Granite is a hard, crystalline, acid rock and produces thin, infertile soil. This is covered with heather and gorse on which sheep and ponies graze and is little use for farming. The lower slopes are more fertile, with pasture for beef cattle. Dartmoor also has other important uses:

1 Some valleys are dammed to create reservoirs, filled by the heavy rainfall, which supply Plymouth and many of the Devon seaside resorts with water.

2 Granite is made up of several minerals, mainly quartz, mica and feldspar. When granite begins to decompose, feldspar becomes kaolin or china clay. This is excavated and exported for use in the pottery industry. Granite is also quarried for use as a building stone.

3 Dartmoor is still a wild, sparsely inhabited region of great natural beauty, and one of Britain's National Parks. This means that it is protected by law from too much development. However, so many people want to visit Dartmoor that there is pressure on roads, car parking and other amenities.

Features of chalk scenery

Escarpments are lines of hills with a steep (scarp) slope and a gentle (dip) slope, formed when chalk was affected by folding during mountain building periods.

Dry valleys are valleys that have no stream or river in them. Possibly they were formed when the water table was higher, or during the Ice Age when the land was frozen and water could not sink through the chalk.

Springs occur at the base of escarpments where the chalk meets a

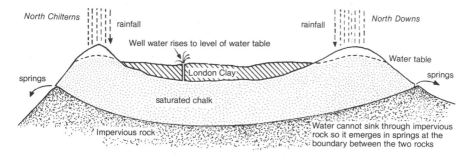

Fig. 5 Cross-section of the London Basin

band of impervious rock or the water table level.

The London basin is an artesian basin (fig. 5). Water collects in the layer of chalk from rainfall on the Chilterns and Downs. When wells are bored through the London clay, the water rises up to the level of the water table.

Features of limestone scenery

1 Dry valleys Most limestone dry valleys are steeper and deeper than those in chalk, sometimes even gorge-like.

2 Scars These are steep slopes where erosion has caused breaking off at a vertical joint.

3 Limestone pavements In areas of level limestone, water attacks and dissolves the limestone along the cracks. The blocks left are called **clints** and the widened joints are called **grykes**.

4 Underground drainage systems As water passes through joints and planes it widens them, sometimes forming large underground caverns. The evaporation of dripping water may leave carbonic deposits which build up to form **stalagmites**, which rise from the floor, and **stalactites**, which hang from the roof. Where the underground water meets the water table at the surface, or at the junction with impervious rocks, the water emerges as springs.

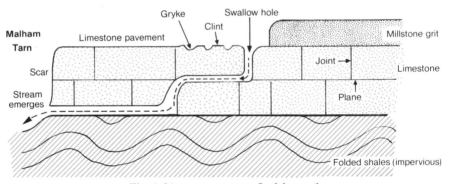

Fig. 6 Limestone scenery, Ingleborough

Summary

1 The earth is made up of layers: the inner and outer core, the mantle and the crust.

2 The crust is made of floating plates. As they move, earthquakes and volcanic eruptions occur.

3 Fold mountains result from the compression of sedimentary layers as plates move together.

4 Igneous rocks are formed from molten magma.

Sedimentary rocks are formed from eroded sediments or the remains of marine animals.

Questions

1 (a) Draw a simple diagram of a rift valley and label the faults, blocks, and fault scarps.
(b) Explain how a rift valley is formed.

2 The following is a description of an important rock:
'This rock, though now at the surface, was formed at great depths below the surface of the earth. It contains large crystals which formed as the original molten rock cooled slowly and solidified.'
(a) Name the rock, an area where it is found, and describe the main features of its landscape.
(b) Why are such areas often sparsely populated?

3 (a) The diagram of an artesian basin, fig. 5, shows a distinctive rock structure. Name this structure.
(b) Explain the term 'water table'.

Aims of this chapter

By the end of this chapter you should know about:

1 The relationships between different elements of the earth's surface.
2 The sculpturing of the surface by weather, rivers, ice and the sea.
3 The economic uses of valleys and coasts.

Ecosystems

System is a word commonly used in Geography. A system consists of a number of elements or parts that are related to and affect one another. The atmosphere, oceans and land surfaces make up a chain of systems. The output of one system is the input of the next.

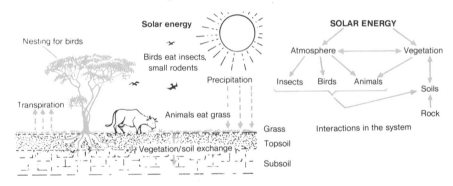

Fig. 1 A temperate ecosystem

Our environment consists of inorganic elements (rocks, subsoil, and atmospheric gases), and organic elements (topsoil, vegetation, bacteria, insects, birds, animals, and human beings). These elements are interdependent, so changes in one element result in changes in others. In the natural world, a balance of elements occurs, but often human activity has interfered with this **ecological balance**. **Ecology** is the study of the interrelationships of the elements, and its pattern in a unit of space is called an **ecosystem**.

Surface drainage

The hydrological cycle

The atmosphere contains water as a result of evaporation from bodies of water, and transpiration from vegetation. The combination of the two processes is called **evapotranspiration**. Water returns to the earth through precipitation. The sequence of processes is called the **hydrological cycle**.

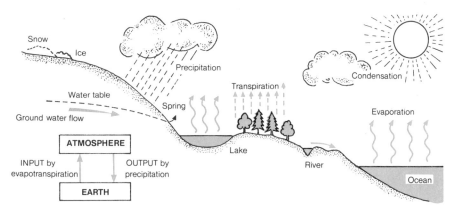

Fig. 2 The hydrological cycle

Evaporation is the conversion of water from its liquid state to its gas state. This requires energy, which is provided in the form of heat. The amount of water evaporated depends on the level of heating and the capacity of the air. When air is holding its maximum amount of water vapour, it is said to be **saturated**.

Transpiration is the process by which vapour is given off by plants, so that they can absorb more moisture from the ground. Rates of transpiration vary. For example, plants in desert regions, where water is scarce, are adapted with special protective surfaces which reduce transpiration.

Drainage patterns

The area drained by streams and rivers that all flow into one major river is called a **river basin**. Its perimeter, the **watershed**, is the boundary between rivers flowing into different river systems. Often, watersheds are formed by mountain ridges or lines of hills.

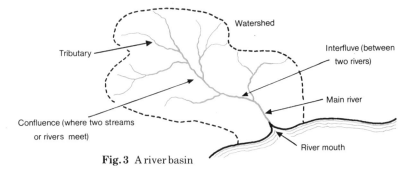

Fig. 3 A river basin

Figure 4 illustrates different patterns of river drainage:

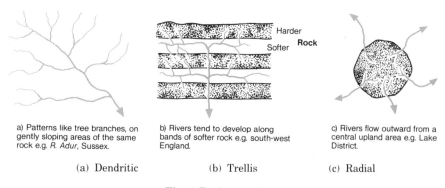

a) Patterns like tree branches, on gently sloping areas of the same rock e.g. *R. Adur*, Sussex.

b) Rivers tend to develop along bands of softer rock e.g. south-west England.

c) Rivers flow outward from a central upland area e.g. Lake District.

(a) Dendritic   (b) Trellis   (c) Radial

Fig. 4 Drainage patterns

Landform processes

The breaking up of the surface is called **erosion**. The movement of eroded material (the load) is called **transportation**, and when that ceases, **deposition** occurs. The main agents of erosion, transportation and deposition, are elements of the weather, rivers, glaciers and the sea. Their action takes various forms, as fig. 5 shows.

Erosion	*Transportation*
Weathering	
1 *Mechanical*	*Mass movement*
Alternate heating and cooling weakens rock, minerals break loose and rocks disintegrate.	1 *Creep*: a very slow movement of weathered material caused by gravity on gentle slopes.
Water in rocks freezes and expands. The pressure causes rocks to shatter. (Freeze-thaw).	2 *Solifluction*: when material is saturated because of poor drainage or heavy rainfall, it moves downslope a few cm. per hour or per day.

Table continues

Erosion	*Transportation*
2 *Chemical* *Solution*: rain-water, or acids in the water, dissolve elements of the rock, e.g. rock salt, limestone. *Oxidation*: oxygen in the atmosphere reacts with rock minerals, e.g. iron and aluminium. *Carbonation*: carbon dioxide combines with minerals, e.g. feldspar forms a soft clay. **3** *Biological*: Root systems exert pressure on surface layers, helping to break up rocks. Burrowing animals expose underlying rocks to air and moisture.	**3** *Earth or mudflows*: a more rapid version of solifluction, occurs on steeper slopes. **4** *Slumping*: the sliding away of part of a slope, e.g. when the slope becomes too steep to support the material. **5** *Landslides*: rapid movement of unstable material triggered off by very heavy rainfall or rapid snowmelt. Great damage can result. **6** *Avalanches*: like landslides but consist mainly of snow rather than rock. Material travels at speeds up to 150 km. per hour and destroys everything in its path. A hazard to skiing and rock climbers.
Rivers and seas **1** *Solution*: dissolving material in the water. **2** *Hydraulic action*: the force of the water. **3** *Corrosion*: the action of particles carried by the water on the bed and edge. **4** *Attrition*: the wearing down of particles in the water as they collide.	**1** *Saltation*: larger particles being bounced along the bed. **2** *Solution*: when material is dissolved in the water. **3** *Suspension*: when the material is carried along in the water. **4** *Traction*: when material is dragged along the bed.
Ice-sheets and glaciers **1** *Plucking*: as ice moves, surface friction causes slight melting. Water penetrates cracks, freezes and expands, loosening rocks which become attached to the ice and dragged along. **2** *Abrasion*: plucked material rubs against the surface causing more erosion.	**1** *Bed-load*: carried along underneath the ice. **2** *Suspended load*: carried on the surface and sides of the ice.

Fig. 5 Erosion and transportation processes

Rivers

The actions of a river are related to its volume and speed of flow. Speed depends on the volume of water and the gradient of the slope. Throughout its course, a river is balancing its energy input and output. A river gains energy from the volume and force of the water, and loses it by friction with the land surface.

Most of a river's energy is absorbed by the movement of water over the river bed, but if there is any surplus, erosion and transportation take place. When there is a deficit, the river reduces its energy requirement by depositing some of the material being carried.

K

At each point, a river is trying to maintain an **equilibrium** between energy input and output. The means of balancing energy will vary according to the nature of the land over which the river is passing. A **long profile** of a river is produced, with the gradient steepest near its source and levelling off towards the sea.

Features of rivers

Feature	Formation
Waterfalls	See fig. 7.
Rapids	See fig. 7.
Potholes	Caused by swirling water moving pebbles which wear holes in the river bed.
Meanders	Bends in rivers, see fig. 8.
Oxbow lakes	As meanders grow, the loops become larger. Eventually the river may cut across the neck of the meander, leaving an oxbow lake. Often the lake silts up, leaving a meander scar.
Braiding	Deposition occurs on the river bed, causing the river to split into two or more channels.
Flood plains	The result of river deposition, when some of the load is deposited as alluvium to form a fairly level plain. Flood plains are small in most upland sections of a river, but close to the mouth may be several kilometres wide.
Levées	In its lower reaches, a river may deposit so much alluvium along its sides that banks (levées) are formed. Many of the rivers draining into the Wash have levées.
Terraces	The remains of former flood plains through which the river has cut, e.g. along the Rhine Valley (fig. 14 in chapter 1).
Deltas	See fig. 9. Streams entering a lake often develop a lacustrine delta. Where a smaller river joins a larger one, it often forms a delta-like feature called an alluvial fan.

Table continues

Feature	Formation
Estuaries	Formed where the level at a river mouth is low enough for the sea to enter at high tide. Deposition occurs, which is often exposed as mudflats or sandbanks at low tide. The main channel of the river winds through the estuary.
Rias	The lower reaches of upland river valleys are drowned through a rise in sea level, e.g. Milford Haven.

Fig. 6 The formation of river features

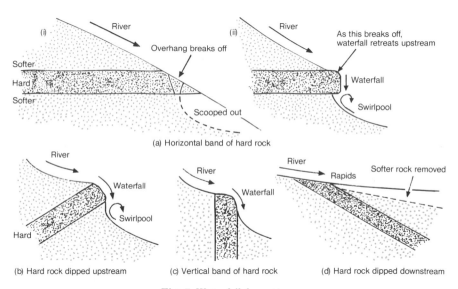

Fig. 7 Waterfall formation

River currents travel in straight lines and, where the river is not straight, they are deflected by the bank. The force of the current eats into the bank so that it is eroded and steepened. The circular action of the current within the river further increases erosion on the outer bank. The eroded bank is called a **bluff**, and when it is very steep, a **river cliff**. On the opposite side of the river the current is much slacker, so deposition occurs, forming a **slip-off slope**. Gradually the loop of the meander becomes larger and migrates upstream.

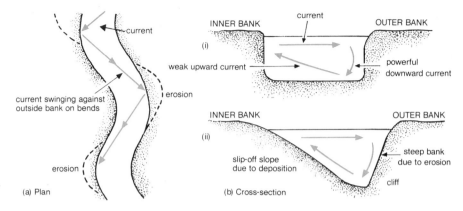

Fig. 8 Formation of meanders

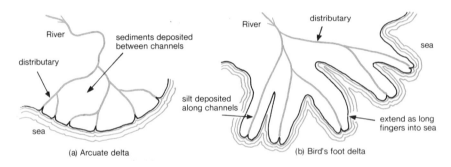

Fig. 9 Delta formations: (a) Arcuate delta; (b) Bird's foot delta

Valleys

The major landform created by a river is the valley in which it flows.
River valleys have three sections:

1 The upper reaches (youthful section). The volume of water is
relatively small, but gradients are steep. Erosion is more important
than deposition, with the river cutting down into its bed
(downcutting, or vertical erosion). The river bed has many boulders,
with shallow and fast-flowing sections called **riffles**, alternating with
deeper slower-moving sections called **pools**. From these, meanders
begin to develop. The valleys often have steep-sloping sides, with
weathered debris at the base. The sides tend to protrude as **spurs**
and when the river winds between their bases they are called
interlocking spurs. These spurs are gradually worn back and become
the less dominant **bluffs**. Features like waterfalls, rapids, lakes and
gorges are likely to be found. **Gorges** are valleys with a narrow
bottom and steep, almost vertical sides, e.g. Grand Canyon, USA.

2 The lower reaches (old-age section). The valley is usually very wide, with a large flood plain, often several kilometres wide, over which the river meanders in huge curves. Features like oxbow lakes and levées tend to be found here. Often the course shifts, and in places the river may be braided. There is some lateral (sideways) erosion, but deposition is far more important than in the upper reaches.

3 Between the upper and lower reaches is a zone which shares some features of each (**maturity**). The valley is wider than in the higher reaches, and spurs have disappeared. Meanders and flood plains have developed, though these are smaller than in the lower reaches. Both erosion and deposition are important. Erosion tends to be lateral rather than vertical.

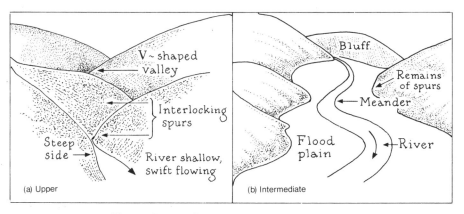

Fig. 10 River valleys: (a) Upper, (b) Intermediate

Use of valleys

Rivers and valleys have been very important to human activity, in agriculture, settlement and communications (see fig. 13 of chapter one).

1 Agriculture In upland regions, valleys are most useful to farmers. Along the valley floors the land is more level, soil is thicker and there is more protection from wind. Flood plains are often fertile, because of their alluvial soils, but their dampness makes them more suitable for pasture than for growing crops. They are the main regions of the world where beef cattle are fattened and dairying takes place. In zones of low rainfall the river is an important source of water for irrigation.

Most of Egypt has an annual rainfall below 250 mm., so that large areas of the country are desert. However, a narrow strip of the country is fertile, highly productive and densely populated, due to the River Nile. This valley is one of the oldest irrigated regions in the world. Until the construction of the Aswan High Dam, the river flooded after heavy rainfall at its source in Central Africa and deposited fertile alluvium. Farmers planted seeds and used methods like the **shaduf** to lift the water from the river on to their fields. Rice is grown in the delta region, otherwise the main crops are cotton, maize, wheat and vegetables.

Since the construction of the Aswan High Dam, the pattern has changed. Larger areas are irrigated with water carried by canal from Lake Nasser. Electricity is produced at the dam by harnessing the force of the water. However, there have been many problems. Alluvium is no longer deposited, so more fertilizer is needed to maintain crop yields. The large extent of irrigation channels has encouraged the spread of water-borne diseases, particularly bilharzia, a tropical disease carried by a small worm that thrives in rivers, lakes and canals.

2 Settlement Much settlement occurred in valleys, because water was available and land was suitable for farming. Many British towns developed at fords or the lowest bridging points of rivers, e.g. York. Settlement tended to be on the higher ground, on the valley sides or on gravel or sandy terraces where drainage was better and there was less risk of flooding.

3 Communications Rivers have always been important routeways. Before the Romans, river transport was the best way of travelling in many areas of Britain. Even today, the major rivers of the world carry a heavy traffic. More important, however, is the use of river valleys as routeways for road and rail communications. Two of the major routeways of Europe occur along river valleys, the Rhône-Saône in France and the Rhine in West Germany. Motorways, railways and pipelines run alongside these rivers, carrying an immense traffic.

4 Pollution Many industries are sited in riverside locations because of the water supply and for communications. Unfortunately, many of these industries discharge their waste into the rivers, although most developed countries have laws to control this to prevent poisons such as lead and mercury being absorbed by fish and killing off river life. An example of accidental pollution was the explosion at a chemical plant in Switzerland in 1986, which poisoned the Rhine.

The use of fertilizers can affect rivers, because surface water drains from fields and rivers. In some parts of the world, raw sewage is pumped into rivers, destroying river life and aiding the spread of water-borne diseases like typhoid, dysentery, cholera and hepatitis. Water for domestic use can be purified by adding chlorine, but this itself can have harmful side-effects.

Ice and the landscape

The period of maximum ice cover occurred over one million years ago during what we call the **Ice Age**. Huge ice sheets covered the mountain areas and the northern lowland areas of Europe, Asia and North America, and glaciers extended to the lowlands further south. The ice has now retreated, so that only the highest regions and latitudes are still covered.

Glacial features

Evidence of glacial erosion is not seen until the ice has melted. Both ice sheets and valley glaciers erode in a similar way but the features produced are much more striking in valleys. Ice sheets tend to scrape the surface of the land, removing soil and loose material, and rounding rock surfaces.

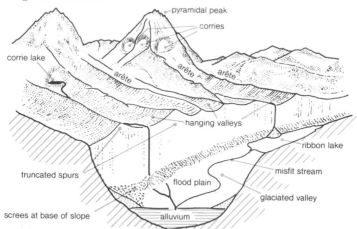

Fig. 11 Main upland glacial features

Most deposition by glaciers and ice sheets occurred on their edges. Some material was left where there was friction along valley sides, but most was deposited as ice melted. As ice retreated, successive bands of material were left.

Feature	Formation
	Features of erosion
Striations	Scratches on the surface of the rock, caused by rocks embedded in the base of the moving ice.
Roches moutonnées	Rocky hummocks that the ice has smoothed on one side and plucked at on the lee side.
Corries (also called cirques or cwms)	Formed by ice in a hollow on a mountain side. As the depth of ice increased, pressure built up and ice began to move downslope, plucking and abrading the back wall of the hollow to create a vertical back, like an armchair.
Corrie lakes	Because the back of a corrie is deeper than the lip, water often remained after the ice melted.
Glacial troughs (U-shaped valleys)	As ice moved from corries, it deepened and widened valleys by plucking and abrasion, to produce a vertical-sided and flat-bottomed feature. After the ice melted, the steep sides were attacked by weathering. The loose material gathered at the base of the valley side to form screes.
Hanging valleys	Larger glaciers had more erosive power and produced deeper valleys than smaller glaciers. When they melted, the tributary valleys were left perched high up on the sides of the main valley.
Truncated spurs	Glaciers in their progress along old river valleys often removed (truncated) the lower parts of the valley spurs.
Rock barriers	Harder bands of rock in the path of glaciers were eroded less than the softer rocks, so remained as barriers after the ice melted.
Rock hollows	Softer rock that was eroded more deeply.
Ribbon lakes	As the ice retreated, water collected in lakes behind rock barriers and moraines, or in hollows along the valley floor. Many glacial valleys once held ribbon lakes which drained, leaving flat valley floors.
Arêtes	Thin knife-edged ridges left between the sides of two corries.
Pyramidal peaks	When several corries formed on the sides of a mountain and reduced it to a fragment of its original, like Snowdon.
Fjords	Ice deepened some valleys so much that the sea flooded them after the ice melted. Fjords are deeper at the landward end, with a shallow threshold to the sea. The west coast of Norway is a famous region of drowned glacial valleys, e.g. Sogne Fjord.

Table continues

Feature	Formation
	Features of deposition
Till	Material dumped by the ice, a mixture of large and small boulders and clay, often called boulder clay.
Moraines	Heaps of material left by melting ice. Four main kinds: lateral moraines along valley sides, medial moraines at the junction of two valleys, terminal moraines at the snout of the glacier or the edge of the ice sheet, and ground moraines left underneath the ice.
Drumlins	Great mounds of material streamlined by the passage of the ice sheet to form smooth, oval shaped hills up to 30m high.
Erratics	Large boulders moved from their original site by the ice and deposited from one to several hundred kilometres away.
Outwash deposits	In front of the ice sheets, meltwater deposited silt, sands and gravels over low-lying areas beyond the ice sheet.
Eskers	Streams flowed underneath glaciers and formed tunnels, which sometimes became choked with debris. After the ice melted they remained as long ridges of material in the shape of the tunnel's path.
Kames	When streams emerged from tunnels at the edge of the ice, their speed slackened and sand and gravel was deposited as a delta in a fan shape.

Fig. 12 Formation of glacial features

Human activity in glaciated landscapes

Many glaciated regions of the world are inhospitable. The combination of cold climates due to latitude or altitude, and mainly acid rocks, has not attracted much settlement. The ice sheets removed most of the topsoil in regions like the Canadian Shield. However, the deepening of river valleys and deposition on their floors has allowed their use for agriculture. The valley floors in some of the mountain ranges, for example in the Austrian and Swiss Alps, are intensively farmed. **Fjord farming** is important in Norway. Cultivation takes place on the lower slopes and cattle are grazed on the higher pastures, or **saeters**. To make an adequate living, the Norwegian fjord farmers are also foresters and fishermen.

Some glacial features are an important resource for tourism. The presence of ribbon lakes in Cumbria has helped to make the Lake

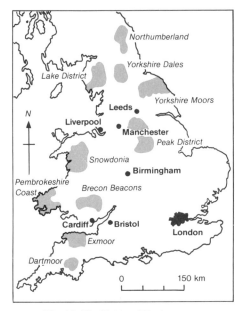

Fig. 13 The National Parks

District the most popular tourist region of Britain (see fig. 12 in chapter 1).

The Lake District became a National Park following the National Parks Act of 1949, and suffers from a conflict of land uses. Millions of visitors threaten the preservation of the natural environment, and so there is a special conservation board, the Lake District Special Planning Board. This Board places strict planning controls on new building, on the ways in which the Forestry Commission develop forests and on the use of the mountains and lakes for recreation.

Coasts

Material is transported along a coastline by **longshore drift**. This is shown in fig. 14. The material is deposited when conditions change, e.g. where there is a barrier, a slackening of current, or a change in the angle of the coast.

Fig. 14 Longshore drift

Land

Beach

Sea

oblique waves

wind

→ Swash : moves material along beach

---→ Backwash: takes material back downslope

Feature	Formation
	Features of erosion
Headlands and bays	Where bands of resistant and less resistant rock alternate, the latter are worn away to form bays separated by headlands of resistant rocks, e.g. along the coast of South Devon.
Cliffs	Wave action at the base of the land causes a notch to be cut. Eventually the overhang is weathered away, leaving a sharp face. The slope of the cliff face usually depends on the angle of the layers or bedding planes, e.g. the 'white cliffs' of Dover.
Wave-cut platforms	The cliff face retreats as erosion continues, leaving a fairly level area of rock which is exposed at low tide, e.g. Nash Point, South Glamorgan.
Caves	The sea attacks weaknesses in the cliffs like joints, faults and cracks and widens them to form caves, e.g. Paviland Caves.
Blow holes	Occasionally the pressure of air compressed in caves by waves weakens the roof, so that blow holes form.
Sea arches	When two caves from each side of a headland meet, e.g. Durdle Door, Dorset.
Sea stacks	Left when spans of sea arches collapse, e.g. The Needles, off the Isle of Wight.
Sea stumps	Eroded sea stacks.
	Features of deposition
Beaches	The main feature of coastal deposition. Vary from tiny beaches in inlets, e.g. along the coast of North Cornwall, pebbly beaches, e.g. Hastings, to long sweeps of sand exposed at low tide, e.g. Blackpool.
Storm beaches	A ridge of boulders, rocks and pebbles at the landward side of a beach, caused by heavy seas and strong tides piling up boulders at the high-tide mark.
Spits	Strips of sand or pebbles extending from one side of a bay, deposited where tides meet with the calmer waters of the bay or inlet, e.g. Orford Ness, Suffolk.
Bars	Spits extending across a bay and closing it off, leaving the water behind as a lagoon, e.g. along the north German coast. If the lagoon drains, a sea marsh is left.
Tombolos	When ridges of deposited material join islands to the mainland, e.g. Chesil Beach, which stretches nearly 30 km from Bridport to the Isle of Portland, separating The Fleet from the English Channel.

Fig. 15 Formation of coastal features

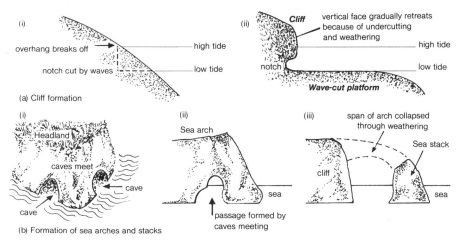

Fig. 16 Features of coastal erosion

Economic uses of coasts

1 Tourism: in Europe, more holidays are spent by the sea than in any other environment.

2 Ports developed in favoured coastal locations where there is deep water and protection from the elements.

3 Heavy industries favour coastal sites because there are large stretches of level land, raw materials can be imported easily, and land is often cheaper. Among the modern industrial plants that have coastal locations in Britain are iron and steel-making, oil refining and power production.

Coastal industries

1 South Wales is an important steel-making area. There are two large integrated plants, near Newport and at Port Talbot. Both are on the coast with level land and good communications. Iron ore and oil are brought by sea, coal comes from the nearby coalfield by rail or motorway, and limestone is quarried locally.

2 South Wales also has a major oil-refining centre at Milford Haven, where there is a deepwater terminal in the ria. Tankers bring crude oil from the North Sea, north and west Africa and the Middle East. It is refined there, or piped to the Llandarcy refinery.

3 Many modern power stations are built near the coast, for easy import of fuel, on sites remote from large towns because of the risk of explosion. Many oil-fired power stations are found close to oil refineries, e.g. Pembroke, near Milford Haven. Sixteen of Britain's seventeen nuclear power stations have coastal sites.

Sea pollution
Waste is discharged into the sea at an even higher rate than into rivers. Smaller seas, like the Mediterranean (sometimes described as an 'open sewer'), cannot absorb all the effluent. Apart from chemical waste and raw sewage, a recent hazard is oil discharged from tankers. Accidents to supertankers can result in huge oil-slicks which affect marine life and destroy bird life. Toxic wastes can kill fish or make them unfit for human consumption. Only proper treatment of chemicals and sewage can reduce the problem.

Summary

1 The landscape is altered by agents of erosion and deposition.
2 The action of rivers is determined by volume and gradient. Erosion takes place when there is an excess of energy, and deposition when there is a deficit. Rivers have steep-sided narrow valleys in the upland reaches, and wide valleys with extensive flood plains and huge meanders in the lower reaches.
3 Ice moulds the upland landscape producing glacial troughs and associated features, and many lowland areas are covered by glacial and outwash deposits.
4 The sea attacks the coastline to produce features such as cliffs, caves, sea arches, headlands and bays. Material is moved by longshore drift and forms beaches and spits.
5 Coasts are important for tourism, for freight movement and for heavy industry.

Questions

1 Study fig. 10 on page 43.
(a) Describe four differences between the upper valley and the intermediate valley.
(b) Explain one of the differences you have described.
2 Many river valleys have been subjected to large-scale human activity. Give a named example of a river valley where there has been extensive urban or industrial development, and explain how this has affected the natural development of the river and its valley.
3 Name a river or lake in the UK where the purity of water has been destroyed by human action. Explain three ways in which pollution has occurred there.
4 (a) Draw a labelled diagram of cliff formation.
(b) Name four uses for a stretch of level coastline that may be in conflict with one another.

5 Understanding weather and climate

Aims of this chapter

By the end of this chapter you should know about:

1 The elements of climate: heat, water, pressure, and winds.
2 Weather patterns like depressions and anticyclones.
3 The analysis of weather maps, satellite photographs and climate graphs.
4 Factors affecting climate.
5 Weather hazards.

Heat

Heat is a major element of climate. Its main source is the sun. The transfer of heat is called the **energy budget**.

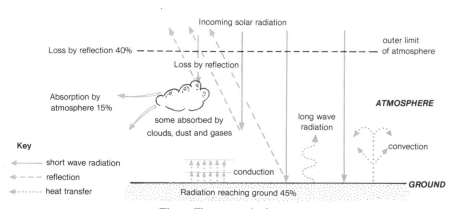

Fig. 1 The energy budget

Temperature is a measure of heat, recorded by a thermometer. When the temperature rises, mercury expands along the tube of a thermometer, and when it falls the mercury contracts. Highest and lowest temperatures over a period of time are measured using a maximum and minimum thermometer. They are placed in a Stevenson's Screen, which is a white box with slatted sides supported on four legs at a height of one-and-a-half metres.

Look at your course books to revise meteorological instruments. You need to be able to recognize maximum and minimum thermometers, a hygrometer, a rain gauge, a barometer and an anemometer.

Water

The hydrological cycle is described on page 37.

Humidity is the term given to the amount of moisture in the air, and is measured by a wet and dry bulb hygrometer. When the humidity of the air is 100 per cent, the air is said to be **saturated**.

Condensation occurs when vapour is converted to a liquid or solid state. Normally it results from a drop in temperature. The temperature at which water vapour condenses is called the **dew point.** This varies according to the amount of water vapour in the air. The dew point occurs at a higher temperature in saturated than in dry air. Condensation is aided by the presence of tiny particles of salt or dust, around which droplets form.

Types of condensation

Type	*Formation*
Dew	Droplets of water deposited on the surface of the ground, commonly formed in spring and autumn during nights with clear skies.
Frost	Formed in the same way as dew, but the water vapour condenses into fragments of ice because of lower temperatures.
Fog	Occurs when the temperature of the air above the ground falls below dew point and droplets remain suspended in the air.
Radiation fog	Forms in low-lying areas and valleys where still, cold air is trapped, e.g. when there is great heat loss because of clear night skies.
Advection fog	Forms when warm air meets cold air or a cold surface. At the junction, the temperature falls and condensation occurs.
Mist	A less dense form of fog.
Clouds	Water vapour condensed into millions of tiny water droplets and ice particles in the air. Clouds develop at different levels and are an indicator of weather. High

Table continues

Type	Formation
	clouds are called *cirrus*, low clouds *stratus*, and storm clouds *cumulonimbus*. Clouds form when warmer air meets colder air, when air is forced to rise over high land and cools (orographic), or in convection currents, because air cools as it rises.
Precipitation (rain, drizzle, sleet, snow and hail)	Occurs when enough condensation has taken place. The result of air of different temperatures meeting, of air forced to ascend over mountains, or rising and cooling through convection.
Hail	Hailstones are produced in convection clouds when the air rises and falls very rapidly.
Snow	Precipitation in its solid state.
Sleet	A mixture of rain and snow. Snow begins to fall, but if the temperature of the lower atmosphere is above freezing, some snow melts before it reaches the ground.

Fig. 2 Types of condensation

Pressure and wind

The atmosphere exerts **pressure** due to the weight of the air. As air is heated, it expands and becomes less dense, so it exerts less pressure. When air cools it contracts and becomes more dense, so it exerts more pressure. Pressure is higher near the ground, and falls with distance from the ground. Pressure is measured by a **barometer**, recorded in millibars and shown on weather maps by **isobars** (lines joining places with equal pressure).

Pressure influences wind direction and speed. Wind is the movement of air from one place to another. Air moves towards areas of low pressure and away from areas of high pressure. The strength

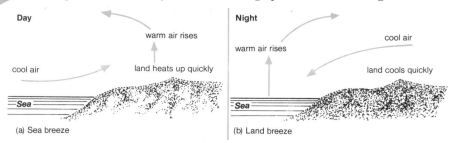

Fig. 3 Land and sea breezes

of the movement depends on the pressure gradient. When the pressure gradient is steep, the winds are strong, but when it is slack the winds are light. Local winds are the result of the shape of the land. On mountain sides, air moves downslope in the day and upslope at night, due to temperature variations. At the coast, land and sea breezes are due to land heating more quickly than the sea during the day, and the sea cooling more slowly than the land at night.

A wind vane shows the direction of the wind. The speed of the wind is measured by an anemometer, and recorded in knots. The Beaufort Scale has points 1 to 12 to indicate the strength of the wind. Force 0 is calm, force 8 is a gale and force 12 is a hurricane.

Weather patterns

A number of weather systems can be recognized by pressure and weather.

A **depression** is an area of low pressure. In north-west Europe, fronts are usually associated with low pressure. Two air masses meet, one of tropical origin, the other of polar origin, and because they do not mix easily, there is a well-defined boundary called a **front**. This boundary is not a straight line, but has bulges and waves along it. What often happens is that the warm tropical air advances northward, pushing a wedge into the polar air. As this occurs, the pressure falls, and a depression begins to develop. Once formed, the depression moves eastwards and a closed system of isobars develops around it.

Ahead of the depression is the **warm front** (shown on the weather map by a line with semi-circles), where advancing warm air rises over cold polar air. Behind the warm front is the **warm sector**, of

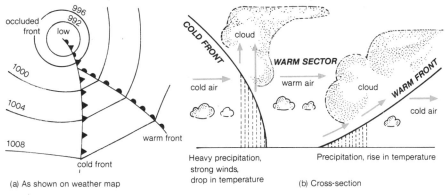

Fig. 4 A depression

mild tropical maritime (oceanic) air. Behind that is the **cold front** (shown by a line with black triangles), where cold air to the rear of the depression is undercutting and lifting the warm air off the ground. Because the cold front moves more quickly than the warm front, it eventually catches it up and lifts the warm air off the surface. At this stage the front is said to be **occluded**, and is shown by alternating semi-circles and triangles.

 An **anticyclone** is an area of high pressure. Anticylones are far larger than depressions and move more slowly. They form from sinking air that warms and dries as it descends. In summer, anticyclonic weather is fine and warm with clear skies. In winter, although it may be clear and sunny, it is often very cold because of heat-loss at night. Frost, or radiation fog, may develop. There are calm conditions in the central parts of anticyclones but around the edge are light winds which blow outwards in a clockwise direction.

 Other weather systems that often occur are troughs and ridges. A **trough** is an area of low pressure between two high-pressure areas. The air is unstable, so showery weather can be expected. A **ridge** is the opposite – an elongated area of higher pressure between two low-pressure areas. The weather is similar to anticyclonic weather, but lasts for less time.

Weather maps

To answer a weather map exam question, you have to learn the symbols and recognize the pattern of isobars. Most weather information is shown at the site of weather stations, which are represented by a circle. The inside of the circle is shaded according to the number of oktas (eighths) of cloud cover. The temperature in degrees Celsius is shown on the top left-hand side. Below that is the symbol for the type of weather. Look up your course book and learn those weather symbols. A line extending from the circle shows the direction the wind is blowing from, and the feathers on the end of the line represent the wind speed – each full feather equals ten knots. A second circle around the station indicates calm.

Figure 4 shows how a depression appears on a weather map. You must be able to identify pressure patterns and describe the weather they bring. To give a weather forecast for a place or region, you must work out which pressure system will affect it. Usually, depressions move eastwards, so you can predict the weather that is likely to occur at a place east of a front or depression.

You should be able to explain why particular weather is occurring. The pressure system should be identified, because it is a likely cause. For example, if a station near a cold front is shown as having eight oktas of cloud, strong winds and rain, you can state that the cold front is responsible.

A satellite photograph may be included as part of a question about weather. Weather patterns can be recognized on these photographs. Areas of high pressure can be identified by the absence of cloud. Depressions show up as the centre of a pattern of spirals, often in a comma shape. This is because the clouds tend to form in bands, tens of kilometres wide. Areas of active convection can be recognized by speckled areas on the photograph. When a weather map is accompanied by a satellite photograph, it is possible to identify the weather patterns by comparing cloud patterns on the photograph with the weather information on the map.

Explaining the weather shown on a weather map or satellite photograph may require additional information. So far, temperature, precipitation, pressure and winds have been described, but there are other factors which can explain differences from one area to another.

Fig. 5 A weather map

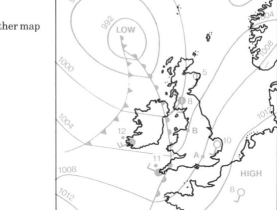

1200 GMT February 20th

Factors affecting climate
The climate of a region is influenced by the prevailing atmospheric conditions (see fig. 6). Wind systems and pressure belts vary over the world, because of the rotation of the earth, and the transfer of heat from hot regions to cooler regions.

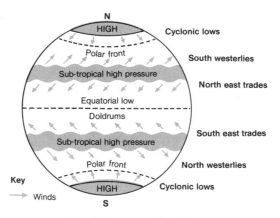

Fig. 6 Planetary circulation

Latitude

Temperatures decrease with increasing latitude, so the closer to the Pole a region is, the cooler its temperature will be. This is particularly so in summer.

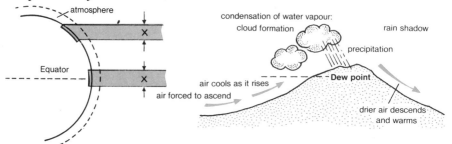

Because of the curvature of the earth, x amount of radiation has a smaller area to heat at the Equator than in higher latitudes. Also at the Equator the distance through the atmosphere is shorter so less heat is lost.

Precipitation caused by air rising over mountains is called orographic. On the lee side the air is drier and warmer, giving a rain shadow effect.

(a) Effect of latitude　　　　　　　　　　(b) Effect of altitude

Fig. 7 How latitude and altitude affect climate (a) Effect of latitude (b) Effect of altitude

Altitude

The pattern of temperature decrease due to latitude is modified by altitude. There is a fall in temperature with height; the average rate of heat loss with ascending height is 6.5°C per 1km. Thus mountain areas have lower temperatures than the lowlands around them. Precipitation is also affected.

Distance from the sea

K Large expanses of water affect climate. Water warms more slowly than the land, because there is a greater volume to be heated, and for the same reason it cools more slowly. So coastal areas are cooler than inland areas in summer, and warmer in winter. The sea has a moderating effect, producing a more equable climate.

K The existence of a large land mass affects climate, because it is a source of cold air in winter and warm air in summer. Extremes of temperature are experienced in continental areas, because of the distance from seas.

Precipitation is affected by distance from the sea, for the oceans are the major source of water for the atmosphere. As air passes over open water, it absorbs moisture, and when the air is cooled, precipitation is likely to occur. Therefore coastal areas have higher precipitation totals than inland areas. The further inland an area is, the less precipitation it receives. Most of the driest areas of the world occur in the interior of continents where there is high pressure.

The climate of the British Isles

All the foregoing factors produce the climate we experience in Britain. Figures 9 and 10 in chapter one show the pattern of temperatures and the distribution of precipitation over the British Isles.

Temperatures decrease northwards in summer, due to the effect of latitude. In winter, the pattern is of west-east decrease, because of the influence of the sea. To the west of the British Isles, the North Atlantic Drift brings the warmer water of the tropical regions northwards. This warms the air, so that when the prevailing westerly winds are blowing, milder air is brought to the western side of the British Isles. As this air continues to move eastwards, it is cooled by contact with the land, so that temperatures in the east are lower. Variations to the main temperature pattern are the result of relief: mountain areas are cooler that the surrounding lowlands.

Precipitation totals are higher in the west than in the east. Most precipitation is brought by westerlies after their passage over the North Atlantic. Most of the uplands of the British Isles are in the west, so precipitation is higher there, while the lowland areas to the east are in the rain-shadow area. The greatest amounts of snow occur in the north, the east and on the mountains where temperatures are lower.

Climate graphs

A climate graph is constructed by plotting average monthly
temperatures of a place and joining these points with a line.
Precipitation is shown by a bar proportional in height to the monthly
total. In fig. 8 there are three climate graphs, each showing a
different climate.

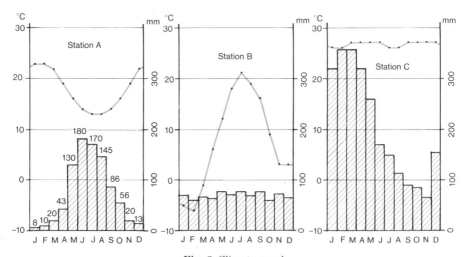

Fig. 8 Climate graphs

From a climate graph, you can find out the highest and lowest
temperatures and the precipitation totals, and when they occur. You
can calculate the range of temperature (i.e. the difference between
the highest and lowest temperature), and the total precipitation.
Climate graphs show the general pattern of climate thoughout the
year. Equable climates have only small variations, but extreme
climates have very marked differences in temperature and
precipitation. If the warmest months recorded are December,
January or February, it means that the weather station is in the
southern hemisphere.

The hazards of the weather

A **hazard** is a situation likely to cause damage to people, property
and the environment. Climatic hazards are a combination of the
physical event itself and the nature of the society that is affected.

For example, a blizzard in Britain may paralyse transport very quickly, but the same amount of snow falling on an Alpine city like Innsbruck will be accepted as normal.

Hazards frequently cause not only expensive damage, but loss of life (see fig. 4 in chapter 1). The poorest parts of the world and the weakest members of society are most at risk. In Bangladesh, millions of poor people live in river delta areas prone to flooding. Nearer home, it is babies and old people who are most likely to die in cold winters, because they are more vulnerable to hypothermia, a condition caused by severe lowering of the body temperature when living in an inadequately heated environment.

Types of hazard

1 Floods occur after very heavy or persistent rain, during rapid snowmelt, when high tides inundate low-lying coastal areas, or when dams or river banks collapse. One of the most terrifying flood situations sometimes occurs after an underwater earthquake has generated an enormous wave, or tsunami. This can race towards the shore and completely swamp flat coastal plains, leaving little time for escape.

2 Tropical cyclones (sometimes called hurricanes or typhoons) are intense, low pressure vortexes, surrounded by winds of at least 33 m. per second. About 80 tropical cyclones occur annually, causing the loss of about 20,000 lives. The most disastrous storms have affected the Bay of Bengal coasts of India and Bangladesh.

3 Tornadoes are violent, whirling vortexes of rising air, producing a funnel-shaped cloud above. The typical tornado damage path is 150 m. wide and up to 10 km. long. In the USA, they are most likely to occur in May; in 1974 a single tornado killed 307 people.

4 Drought is lack of water, but the definition of drought varies greatly. For example, there was a serious drought in the mid-1970s in the UK when, for eighteen months, rainfall was only half the normal. Even so, there was much more rain than would be expected in the Sahel under normal conditions.

Droughts cannot be prevented, but reactions to them vary. Poorer countries do not have the capital resources to reduce the impact of drought by expanding water storage schemes, so it is often necessary for international organizations like the Red Cross to bring in food supplies. Even so, resources have not been sufficient to prevent starvation during the African famine caused by the Sahel drought.

In the developing countries of the drought-prone regions of the world, a farmer's wealth is often measured by the number of livestock he owns. As a result, in many north African countries the land is over-stocked in relation to the grazing and fodder available.

Through over-grazing, the vegetation disappears, and desert-like conditions spread, a process known as **desertification**. This process can also happen in developed countries, as in the 'Dust Bowl' in the mid-west of the USA in the 1930s. Today, parts of eastern England are at risk. Hedgerows have been removed and extensive arable farming methods can expose the soil to the destructive elements of the weather. During dry weather in March, strong winds can remove topsoil exposed by winter ploughing. Farmers, though, are aware of the need to protect their soil, and are increasingly aware of the ecological value of preserving hedgerows.

5 Pollution Some hazards are the result of human activity. The worst of these stem from pollution. The air is polluted by emissions from industrial processes.

Pollutant	Cause and effect
sulphur dioxide	Created when coal and oil are burned. Power stations are the major source.
carbon monoxide	Comes from vehicle exhausts. In high concentrations it can be fatal.
carbon dioxide	Produced by burning fuels. Screens radiation.
hydrocarbons and **nitrogen oxide**	Produced by vehicle exhausts. Responsible for the smog that can develop in cities like Los Angeles, where summers are hot and sunny.
smoke	Produced whenever fuels are burnt. Industry and the home contribute to the smoke levels of the atmosphere. In Britain the situation was greatly improved by the Clean Air Act of 1956, which banned the emission of dark smoke and allowed local authorities to set up smoke-control districts.

Fig. 9 Types of pollution

Although the air is now cleaner, there is little legislation to control vehicle fumes and the sulphur dioxide given off by power stations. Gradually, the use of lead in petrol is being phased out but the atmospheric effects of sulphuric acid need far more attention. Sulphur dioxide in the atmosphere dissolves in water droplets to form sulphuric acid. This increases the acidity of rain. **Acid rain** is having very serious effects. In many parts of Germany and

Scandinavia the trees are dying and fish are disappearing from the lakes and rivers. Half of West Germany's forest cover has been affected, and in southern Norway 10 000 sq. km. of lakes have lost their fish population. Since the prevailing winds over Europe are south-westerly, emissions from British power stations are contributing to the acidity of the rain falling on our European neighbours. Over four million tonnes of sulphur are emitted in Britain, of which as much as 60 000 tonnes is estimated to fall on Norway each year.

Summary

1 The sun heats the earth by short-wave radiation and the earth heats the atmosphere by long-wave radiation.

2 The atmosphere gains water from the ground by evapotranspiration and returns it as precipitation.

3 Depressions are areas of low pressure, often with fronts, that bring unsettled conditions and heavy precipitation. Anticyclones are areas of high pressure bringing clear skies and calm weather, warm in summer, cold in winter.

4 The planetary circulation, latitude, altitude and distance from the sea are the main factors affecting climate.

5 Temperatures in the UK decrease from south to north in summer, and from west to east in winter. Rainfall is highest in the west and on the mountains.

6 Weather causes many hazards, including cyclones, floods, droughts, gales and heavy snowfall. Human activity can be a further hazard, by polluting the air.

Questions

1 Study the weather map in fig. 5 on page 57.
(a) What is the pressure at Point A?
(b) Draw the symbols for (i) the warm front, (ii) the cold front.

(c) Name the pressure systems affecting (i) Ireland, (ii) north-west Europe.

(d) Describe the sequence of weather you would expect at Point B over the next 24 hours.

2 Study the climate graphs in fig. 8 on page 60.

(a) Which example is taken from the southern hemisphere? Give one reason for your answer.

(b) What is the annual total precipitation for Station A?

(c) What are the maximum and minimum temperatures for Station B? In which months do they occur?

(d) Name the type of climate found at Station C. Give two reasons for your answer.

3 (a) Name one hazard that is more common in tropical latitudes, and one that is more common in temperate latitudes.

(b) For one of the hazards you have named, suggest two ways in which its effects can be reduced.

Aims of this chapter

After reading this chapter, you should understand:

1 The factors affecting the distribution of population.
2 The terms 'over-populated' and 'under-populated'.
3 How to analyse birth and death rates.
4 How to construct a population pyramid and identify different population structures and their causes.
5 The different types and causes of migration.

The distribution of people

The population of the world is not evenly spread. It is concentrated into a number of regions, while the remainder of the world is sparsely inhabited, as fig. 1 shows. Population can be measured by total, or by calculating its density. **Density** of population refers to the number of people in a given area. For example, the population of the UK is 56 020 000 and its area is 244 100 sq. km. The population is divided by the area to give a population density of 230 per sq. km.

Factors affecting the distribution of population

There are many reasons for the uneven distribution. Figure 2 gives a summary of the main types of environment in the world. The main influences are:

1 **Relief** Mountain ranges like the Andes and the Himalayas are sparsely inhabited, because the environment is hostile to settlement (see page 47). The highest population densities are found in areas of fairly level and low-lying ground, mainly river basins and along coasts.

2 **Climate and vegetation** Many parts of the world have unpleasant climates. Certain areas are sparsely settled because the climate is too cold (the polar regions of Asia and North America, and Antarctica), because the rainfall is too low to support agriculture, e.g. the hot deserts, or because the combination of high temperatures and high humidity makes living conditions very uncomfortable.

Most highly populated regions occur where the climate is temperate or tropical but not too humid, or in dry areas where there is a good water supply, e.g. the Nile Valley.

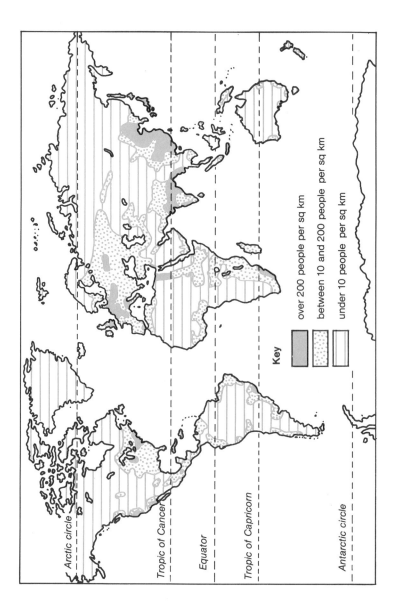

Fig. 1 World population densities

Key

- over 200 people per sq km
- between 10 and 200 people per sq km
- under 10 people per sq km

Arctic circle

Tropic of Cancer

Equator

Tropic of Capricorn

Antarctic circle

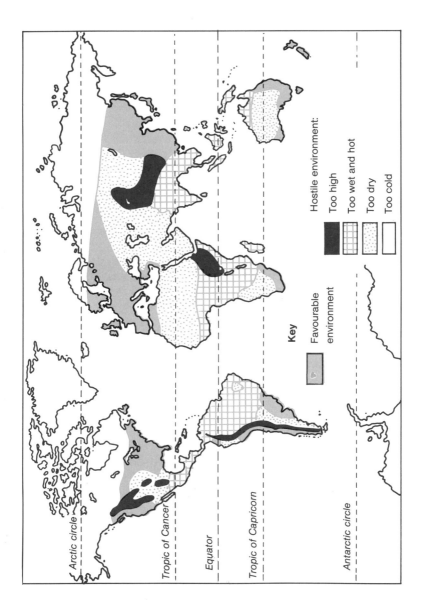

Fig. 2 Hostile and favourable environments of the world

Vegetation has little influence today, because most has been cleared for farming and building, except in the tropical rain forests of Africa and South America, which are very sparsely populated even though the forest cover is being removed rapidly.

3 Resources If there are no resources, there are no means of supporting life. The primary resource is the land which, given warm temperatures for at least part of the year plus an adequate water supply either from rainfall or by irrigation, produces the world's food supply. However, some areas are densely populated because there are other resources to exploit. These resources include minerals, and power for industry.

4 Water supply Fresh water is vital to sustain life. Where there is plenty of surface water and frequent rainfall, as in north-west Europe, population is evenly distributed. Where there is a limited water supply, population is concentrated at points where water is available, as in the river basins of India.

Other factors also help to explain population distribution. These include:

1 **Economy** – the resources of a region and its employment,
2 **Politics** – government policy and regional planning,
3 **Social structure** – the lifestyles of the people.

The distribution of population in the UK

The mountainous regions have low population densities. Relief, soils and climate make farming difficult and in some areas impossible, so in the past, settlement was sparse. The lack of other resources to provide employment helps to explain the low densities today. The main economic uses of the uplands are sheep farming, forestry, water and power supply, recreation and tourism. These are all very important, but they do not create much employment.

Other regions with a fairly low density are rural areas like East Anglia and the South-West. In these regions the physical environment is favourable to agriculture but there is a low demand for labour in modern commercial farming, so population densities are low.

The highest population densities occur in the major urban areas of the UK. Many of the factors that have led to a high population are historical: cities and ports developed in sites which were favourable for communications; the populations of the West Midlands, Merseyside and South Wales increased as manufacturing industry developed.

Today, population is highest in those areas with greatest employment (although it is also high in certain areas of unemployment). Within the cities there are great variations in population density, as fig. 4 shows.

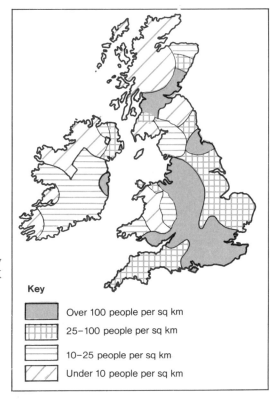

Fig. 3 Population density of the UK

Key

- Over 100 people per sq km
- 25–100 people per sq km
- 10–25 people per sq km
- Under 10 people per sq km

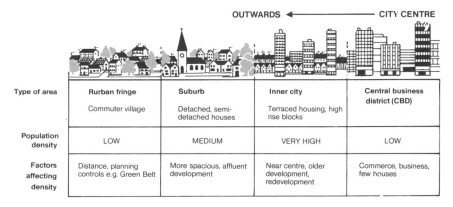

OUTWARDS ◄————————— CITY CENTRE

Type of area	Rurban fringe	Suburb	Inner city	Central business district (CBD)
	Commuter village	Detached, semi-detached houses	Terraced housing, high rise blocks	
Population density	LOW	MEDIUM	VERY HIGH	LOW
Factors affecting density	Distance, planning controls e.g. Green Belt	More spacious, affluent development	Near centre, older development, redevelopment	Commerce, business, few houses

Fig. 4 A section through a typical British city

Social factors are important. The traditional way of life of the upland areas has become less attractive, because many people want a different style of living. High populations may also result from cultural or religious factors. In the cities, the birth rate is high among many of the immigrant communities, because their cultural values encourage large families.

Over-populated and under-populated regions

Over-population occurs when the resources of a region cannot support its population. Regions can have a very dense population, for example parts of the Netherlands, Belgium and West Germany, yet not be over-populated, because of plentiful resources and employment. By contrast, sparsely-populated regions can be over-populated, as for example the Sahel region of Africa, where living standards are very low because there are too many people for the available resources.

However, most of the over-populated regions are also densely populated. These regions are found mainly in the developing world and include Bangladesh, Pakistan, parts of India, parts of South-East Asia, parts of North Africa and the Middle East, and Central America.

Under-populated regions have too few people to exploit the resource potential; development is hampered by the shortage of labour. Often, immigration to these regions has been encouraged. The under-populated regions of the world include parts of Australia and New Zealand, parts of Russia, Scandinavia, and Canada.

Contrasting regional examples

High population in rural areas

The state of Bihar is in North-East India, on the plain of the River Ganges. The average population density is about 267 per sq. km. but along the river it reaches 400 per sq. km. There are several towns, but even the largest, Patna, has a population of only 0.5 million people. The province is mainly rural, with only 10 per cent living in towns.

Intensive farming is the main occupation, and all the land is cultivated. Rice is the most important crop, but millet, maize, lentils, sugar cane, barley and wheat are also grown. Near the rivers there are padi fields, which are small fields surrounded by earth banks called **bunds**. Water is channelled into the fields and the mud is turned by buffalo-drawn wooden ploughs. Young rice plants are then transplanted from nursery beds to the fields. The grain is cut by hand and threshed locally. Often, there are two rice harvests per year. The preparation of the fields, irrigation, and the growing and harvesting of the rice require an enormous amount of labour.

The Bihari people have to be almost self-sufficient. Clothes are produced on hand-looms from raw cotton and pottery is made from river clay, as are the bricks for building. Wood for fuel is collected from the forests.

The fertility of the river soils, and the monsoon climate with high summer temperatures and heavy rainfall, means that there can be more than one harvest per year. The land supports heavy densities of people, but only at a subsistence standard of living. Minor upsets can bring disaster. If the monsoon rains fail (as they did in 1967), there is famine. If there is excessive rainfall, causing flooding, crops and livestock are destroyed.

Rural regions with low population density

1 The Highlands of Scotland, which lie to the north of the Central Lowlands rift valley, have a population density of less than 15 per sq. km. Most of the land is over 200 metres above sea level, with peaks of over 1200 metres in the Grampian and Cairngorm mountains. The rocks are very old, producing soils that are acid, thin and infertile. When the region was glaciated, the topsoil was removed and U-shaped valleys, arêtes and corries were carved out.

The severe climate has summer temperatures rarely over 15°C and winter temperatures averaging only 4° to 5°C, with many days below freezing. Precipitation totals are high in the west, over 2000 mm per year in the higher areas, and snow lies for long periods. The natural vegetation of Scots pine and birch has gone, leaving a vast moorland composed of coarse grasses, heathers and mosses, and peat bogs.

Historically, the environment could only support a small population. The main farming system was **crofting**. Crofts are small rented farms, often not more than four hectares, and crofters supported themselves by grazing sheep on the moorlands, growing winter fodder and vegetables around the croft, and keeping a cow. They supplemented their resources by fishing, by hunting game, by distilling whisky, weaving tweed, and by forestry.

There are still 15 000 crofts, but many crofters have abandoned the land and gone to live in towns like Aberdeen, or have emigrated. New industries have grown up: tourism, power generation, aluminium smelting, and industries associated with offshore oil exploitation. However, none of these industries are large employers, so the population has remained very low.

2 The Amazon Basin is the largest region of Brazil, covering 42 per cent of the total land area, yet containing only five million people, 4 per cent of the country's population. The Amazon is fed by numerous tributaries, carrying alluvium from the Andean ranges, which is deposited in the lowlands. Situated in equatorial latitudes, and low-lying, the Amazon Basin experiences a monotonous tropical climate. Temperature hardly varies throughout the year, averaging about 27°C. Rainfall is high throughout the year, and can be over 2000 mm. per year. As a result, the humidity is very high and this means the climate is difficult to work in. The combination of climate and alluvial deposits supports very dense tropical forest.

The population is mainly found in the few towns, notably Manaus, Belem and Santarem. The rural population has settled along the watercourses, which are both transport links and sources of food. In the interior of the forests a few pure Indian groups are still living by hunting, collecting and fishing, but their numbers are dwindling.

The main resource is the forest itself, but it is difficult to exploit. The Amazon was famous for the production of rubber, but this almost disappeared after rubber plantations were established in Malaysia. There are other economically useful trees, but these are not exploited on a large scale. Mineral resources in the area include manganese, bauxite, iron ore and tin ore. The latter two are not exploited at present, because of the high cost of mining and transport.

Agriculture occurs along the Trans-Amazonian Highway. The native method of farming is **shifting cultivation**: clearing a small area of land, growing crops for a year or two and then abandoning the area for a new one. This system was well adapted to the environment. Settled farming, however, has presented many problems. Despite the warmth, moisture and level land, the region is not very fertile. Heavy rainfall washes the minerals out of the soil, and without a constant supply of humus the soil rapidly loses all goodness. Once cleared of vegetation and ploughed, heavy rains wash away much of the soil. Some crops are cultivated in a small way: manioc, corn and beans. Near the coast, tobacco and pepper are grown commercially.

It seems unlikely that the Amazon region will ever support a very large population, but as forest clearance continues, more people are settling here.

Population changes

By understanding the structure of a population, it is possible to predict changes that are likely to occur.

The **birth rate** is the number of births per 1000 people in a year. The **death rate** is the number of deaths per 1000 people in a year. If

K the birth rate is higher than the death rate, the population is increasing, but if the death rate is higher than the birth rate, then the population is declining. These are termed **natural** increases or decreases.

Many factors affect the birth and death rates of an area or region:

1 The number of women of childbearing age.
2 The proportion in different age groups – elderly, adult, children.
3 The level of medical care.
4 Natural and man-made disasters (famine, earthquakes, wars).
5 Social and cultural behaviour (use of contraception, age of marriage, status of women, etc.)

	Developed world	*Developing world*
Birth rate	11 – 15 per 1000	About 40 per 1000
Factors	Family size limited for economic and social reasons, e.g. maintaining high standard of living, women having a career, high expectations, birth control education.	High infant mortality rate, importance of children as labour and 'insurance' for illness and old age, polygamy, lack of birth control.
Death rate	12 per 1000	Over 20 per 1000
Factors	High medical standards, pure water supplies, sanitation, hygiene, and fewer major natural hazards.	High infant mortality rate, life expectancy is low due to disease, malnutrition, poor medical care and sanitation, polluted water supply, hazards (e.g. floods), wars.

Fig. 5 Contrasts in birth and death rates

Population structure

K **Population pyramids** (see fig. 6), show the structure of a population.

Developed world
The population pyramid shows almost equal proportions of males and females, but more females than males in the oldest age groups because women have a longer life expectancy than men. The totals for each age group gradually diminish with increasing age. This pattern is the result of low birth rates, low death rates and a long life expectancy.

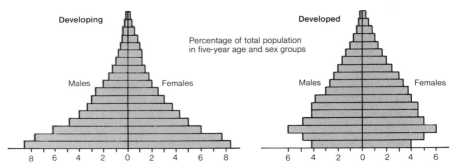

Fig. 6 Population pyramids

Developing world
Because of the high birth rate, the base of the pyramid is very broad, but declines sharply because of the high infant mortality rate. The totals continue to decrease and there are far fewer elderly people. This is because of the high death rate and the low life expectancy.

Variations
Variations in expected patterns may occur for several reasons:
1 Fewer males in the middle age-groups, caused by death in warfare or emigration to work.
2 More males in the middle groups, because employment attracts immigrant workers.
3 Few older age-groups, because of a past war or disaster, like famine or major flooding or disease.
4 Few lower age-groups, because younger people have emigrated, or elderly people have retired there.

Migration

Migration is the term given to the movement of people from one region or place to another. It can be a major cause of population growth or decline in regions.

Causes of migration
Migration is influenced by push and pull factors, as fig. 7 illustrates.

Types of migration
1 **Rural-urban**: this is the most common form of migration. Towns and cities offer more opportunities than the countryside.

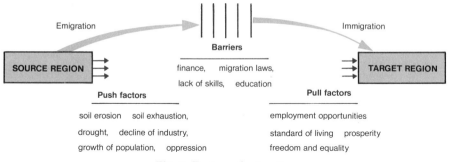

Fig. 7 Factors of migration

Push factors: increased mechanization on farms, so fewer jobs; soil exhaustion; shortage of jobs for younger people; dissatisfaction with agricultural working conditions and lower living standards.

Pull factors: the excitement of city life; the larger number and range of jobs available; opportunities for improvement through education or promotion; a higher standard of living in terms of housing, services and amenities; and more freedom.

2 Urban-rural: this is much less common, and is a feature of the developed rather than the developing world. It is usually a function of good communications which allow people to travel long distances to work. People who prefer to live in a rural environment may move to the country, yet continue to work in the city. This is most common in the USA, where the outward migration of the working population results in higher densities up to about 80 km. from cities like New York and Chicago. This movement contributes to the growth of **conurbations**. A conurbation is a vast urban area made up of several cities and towns.

3 Intra-urban: these are small-scale movements within cities. People move from one city region to another because of redevelopment, or because their needs or income have changed. Because there are distinct housing regions in cities (see fig. 4), people migrate between these regions according to their income and expectations. A rise in income will often lead to a move to a superior level of housing.

4 Inter-urban: this is the movement of people from one city to another. Often the move is from a smaller to a larger city. Reasons include job promotion, work moves within large companies or government services, or because job opportunities are better in the larger cities.

Problems of migration

Many problems are caused by large-scale migration. A big influx of people puts pressure on existing resources, especially in the developing world. High rural birth rates force people to leave the land. They are attracted to the cities, and the unskilled or illiterate are unable to afford housing or find employment. **Shanty towns** develop on the outskirts of such cities in unhealthy, unpleasant places, like the rubbish dumps of El Paso in New Mexico. Settlers collect rubbish, cardboard, and bits of wood to make temporary dwellings. Shanty towns are dangerously overcrowded and there are rarely adequate services. Water has to be carried long distances and there is no sanitation, leading to disease and a high infant mortality rate.

About 75 000 people move from the country to cities throughout the world every day. In South America, over the last 10 years the number of cities with populations over 100 000 has increased from 59 to 116. Possibly the worst situation in the world is found in Calcutta, where there are over 3000 bustees (shanty towns). Disease is rife, especially cholera, smallpox and tuberculosis. The city stretches for 100 km. along the Hooghly River. The density is about 33 000 per sq. km., with over 500 000 people sleeping on the streets. Of the population, less than half were born in Calcutta; many have come from Bangladesh, but the majority come from the rural areas of Bihar (page 70).

A forced exodus from the land, resulting from drought or famine, brings massive problems. Vast numbers of people make their way to the cities, which cannot supply the jobs or food that they need. Often it is only the supply of food from relief agencies that keep the people alive. When the cause is war, some refugees are only temporary, but many are unable to return to their homeland, and are destitute. For example, many large refugee camps in Lebanon are filled with Palestinian Arabs who fled from Israel over twenty years ago.

In the developed world, there is pressure in the depressed inner-city regions where housing is old, often sub-standard, and rents are lower. There are problems associated with even small-scale migration.

Some areas are very popular for retirement, e.g. the south coast of England, towns like Bournemouth. Here the age structure is so top-heavy that it puts great pressure on services like hospitals, doctors and social welfare agencies.

In summary, the problems resulting from migration are as follows:

1 Employment – too few jobs, more competition for existing jobs keeping wage rates low, or migrants not educated or trained for the types of work available.

2 Housing (developed world) – abnormal house price-rises causing financial strain, severe overcrowding in already depressed urban areas; (developing world) – the mushrooming of shanty towns, overcrowding and homelessness.

3 Social provision – social services become over-stretched, particularly in health and education.

4 Services – inadequate services like piped water supply, sewage disposal, resulting in increased health hazards.

5 Transport – pressure on public transport, particularly for the journey to work, traffic congestion and pollution.

K One result of international migration is the formation of **multi-racial** and **multi-cultural** societies. This is a feature of the inner regions of some of Britain's major cities, and extra resources are needed for education and social services. Tension and stress often develop between different immigrant and local communities, which can flare up into violence. Social or economic pressure from outside can trigger racial conflict.

In 1951 there were about 200 000 black people in Britain, but this figure has now increased to two million, of whom about 40 per cent were born in Britain. Immigration controls have now become very strict. The ethnic minority communities are mainly found in the inner city areas of Manchester, Birmingham and London, where over a third of the people are black.

Immigrants often feel like second-class citizens, and after riots in London, Liverpool, Bristol and Birmingham, research has shown that black people do not always have the same opportunities to get jobs, good housing and education as white people.

On the larger scale, migration can lead to oppression, widespread violence, and even civil conflict, e.g. South Africa.

Summary

1 The main factors affecting population distribution are relief, climate, resources and water supply. Economic, political and social factors are also important.

2 In the UK, population is dense in the urban lowland regions and sparse in the upland regions of the north and west.

3 Over-populated regions have too many people for the resources available, and under-populated regions have too few.

4 The birth and death rates (numbers of births or deaths per 1000 people) are used to predict population change.

5 Birth and death rates are affected by medical facilities, water supply, disease, and standard of living and education.

6 Population change may be the result of migration, which is influenced by push and pull factors.
7 There are four types of migration: rural-urban, urban-rural, intra-urban and inter-urban.

Questions

1 Look back to fig. 1, world population density.
(a) Name two countries that have a high density of population.
(b) Give two reasons why most of Africa has a low population density.
(c) Give two reasons why most of Africa has a high birth rate.
2 The table below gives information about the population of various countries.

	Total population in millions	Birth rate	Death rate	Infant mortality rate	People under 15 years	People over 65 years	People in towns
		(per 1000 people)			(percentage)		
UK	56	13	12	13	22	14	76
France	54	14	10	10	23	14	78
Italy	57	12	9	15	22	13	69
USSR	268	18	10	36	26	9	65
India	689	36	15	134	41	3	22
Brazil	121	32	8	84	41	3	61
Nigeria	80	50	18	157	47	2	20

(a) Which country has the highest population?
(b) Which country has the largest proportion living in urban areas?
(c) Which country has the highest rate of natural increase?
(d) The infant mortality rate is the number of babies out of every 1000 born, who die under the age of one. Which country has the lowest rate?
(e) Suggest three ways in which the high death rates of India, Brazil and Nigeria could be reduced.
(f) Give two reasons why India, Brazil and Nigeria have a much lower percentage of people over 65 than the other countries.
3 Select one region that has a low population density. Give three reasons for its low density.
4 Select one region that has a high population density. Give three reasons for its high density.

Aims of this chapter

By the end of this chapter you should know about:

1 The different types of rural settlement.
2 The factors affecting the location of rural and urban settlement.
3 The classification of towns.
4 Land-use zones in cities.
5 The social and economic problems of towns and cities.
6 Urban planning and renewal.

K▶ Settlement can be divided into three types:
1 **Rural** – individual farmsteads, hamlets and villages.
2 **Urban** – towns and cities.
3 **Suburban** – between the totally urban areas and the completely rural areas.

Rural settlement

Types of settlement

Rural settlement may be either nucleated or dispersed. **Dispersed** settlement occurs when farmers occupy houses on their own land, surrounded by fenced or hedged fields. **Nucleated** settlements are where farmhouses are clustered in a village and farmers cultivate strips of land scattered around the village. Nucleated rural settlements are found in most of the lowland areas of the world.

It is rare for settlements to be entirely dispersed. Most common is a mixture of fairly evenly spaced villages with individual farmsteads around. One reason for this is that villages provide services like one or two shops, a bar, possibly a petrol station, and a place of worship.

Most villages are associated with agriculture. However, strung out along coastlines are villages that owe their existence to fishing, while on coalfields and near mineral deposits, mining villages have grown up. In some areas, planned settlement occurs, often on reclaimed land, like in the Netherlands or southern Italy.

K▶ In many mountain areas, there are settlements which are only occupied for a few months each year. These provide shelter for farmers and their families who practise transhumance (see page 102). Temporary settlements are also built by tribes engaged in shifting agriculture, particularly in tropical forest regions. Nomadic peoples, too, may construct temporary dwellings, or carry tents with them, like the Bedouin of North Africa.

Layout of villages

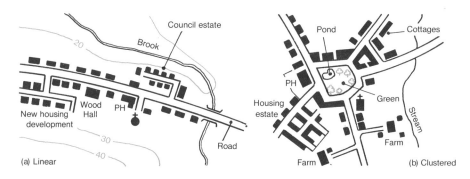

Fig. 1 Village plans (a) Linear (b) Clustered

Recent developments have altered the shapes of villages. Commuting has produced ribbon developments around the villages. Houses are built along the roads leading out of the village.

Why villages grew up
Most settlements developed with farming, many centuries ago. The factors that influenced their location are those of a former age. Today, most communities do not need to be self-sufficient, because of good transport. In the past, however, local supplies of building material, fuel and water were vital, and these continue to be essential in the less-developed parts of the world. The following factors were of primary importance in the location of a village:

1 Land. There had to be enough land to grow crops and graze animals, for feeding and clothing the community. Suitable building land was also needed, which was neither too marshy nor liable to flood, yet not too steep or exposed.

2 Water supply. This had to be close enough to be transported to the settlement. The most common sources of water were springs, streams, rivers and freshwater lakes. In areas of pervious rocks, wells could be sunk. Dependable water supplies were required in regions with summer drought, not only for human and animal use, but also for crop irrigation. Village locations at water sources in areas of limited water supply are called **wet-point** sites.

3 Other resources. The communities needed materials for
building, and a source of fuel, which could be supplied from woods
and forests. In the absence of woodland, other building materials had
to be found. In some regions stone was quarried, in others mud was
baked into bricks, and elsewhere wattle and daub was used. The only
substitutes for wood as fuel, until the discovery of coal, were dried
animal dung (used most in southern regions) and peat.

There have been changes in the rural settlement pattern over the
centuries. The decline and disappearance of some settlements has
occurred because of depopulation, owing to war, famine, disease, soil
exhaustion, or changes in farming systems; and because of changes
in employment, with mechanization of farming and better jobs in
towns causing a drift from the land. The main growth in settlements
has occurred through the growing urbanization of rural areas.

Urban settlement

Types of settlement

Urban settlements can be classified by size or by function. The size
and number of towns depends on the density of population. Areas of
unfavourable relief and countries with few resources have fewer
urban settlements.

Towns have a variety of functions. The most important functions
are those that employ the greatest numbers and earn most of a
town's income. They can be divided into two categories: basic and
non-basic. **Basic** functions relate to the area outside the town, and
earn its income; **non-basic** functions serve the population living in
the town.

Towns act as service centres for the surrounding area. Many towns
have other important functions, like administration, industry,
transport, marketing and tourism. For example, a capital city is
usually the seat of national government, the country's financial
centre, and contains the head offices of the country's major companies
and institutions. In the capitals of the developed world, most
employment is in services, including banking, administration,
transport and tourism.

Why towns grew up

Many types of locations favoured the growth of towns:
1 Markets. In productive farming areas with a surplus of food
production, towns grew up as service centres. At a meeting place of
communications, goods would be exchanged, and gradually trades
developed supplying the farmers with tools and skills.

2 Other historic factors. Towns developed around castles, as people sought protection and a market for their goods and services. Easily defended sites were attractive, and prospered. Politics was an important factor: powerful lords established cities as centres for their administration. Countries that conquered other regions set up towns as trading posts, as ports, or as administration centres from which the region could be controlled and governed.

3 Communications. Towns often grew up at crossroads, bridging points and valley entrances. Traffic which crossed a bridging point, or passed through a valley, brought with it trade. Often settlements would grow up to service those engaged in the exchange of goods. Points at which a change in type of transport occurred also fostered growth, e.g. goods brought overland and transferred to water transport. Coasts and sea ports were particularly important in this respect. The coming of the railways produced new nuclei, or centres, for urban growth.

4 Industry. Many towns grew up or expanded during the period of the Industrial Revolution. On coalfields, coal mining caused the growth of settlements. The industrial network developed and towns expanded, especially coastal towns that exported coal and industrial products. Most of the industrial urban areas are found in the coalfield regions, even where coal is no longer important.

Much urban growth in this century is related to industry. As modern industries have grown, so have their nearby urban centres. Industry does not often produce new towns, but contributes to the expansion of existing towns.

Nevertheless, some new towns have appeared within the last fifty years. Kiruna and Gällivare in northern Sweden are the result of the exploitation of the iron ore deposits. Many new towns have been planned to take population from crowded cities like Paris and London. Other towns have been planned for political reasons, for instance the construction of Brasilia as the new capital of Brazil.

5 Resorts. Towns have grown due to the demand for recreation. The main reason for the expansion of tourism in recent decades has been improvements in transport, especially the advent of the charter flight. People from the developed world have stimulated the growth of holiday resorts in many parts of the developing world, because they can afford to travel long distances to reach places with good climates, beaches, and local interest. The islands of the Caribbean attract Americans, and the Gambian coast in West Africa, for instance, attracts Europeans.

Measuring the importance of towns
The simplest way to measure the importance of urban areas is by population. In the rank/size classification, urban areas are ranked or

listed according to their population. Thus the greater its population, the higher is the rank given to a town. Figure 2 classifies the towns of the UK according to population.

Population (thousands)	
Greater London	6696
Birmingham	920
Glasgow	762
Liverpool	510
Sheffield	477
Manchester	449
Leeds	449
Edinburgh	419
Bristol	388
Belfast	374
Croydon	317
Coventry	314
25 towns between 201 and 300	
51 towns between 101 and 200	

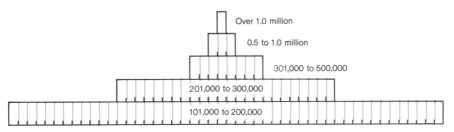

Fig. 2 Ranking of UK towns

In most countries, there are many more small towns than large towns, as in the UK. Figure 2 shows how they form a **hierarchy** when ranked. Countries like the UK have a pyramid-like hierarchy, but other countries may be unbalanced, with a very dominant capital city, called a **primate** city.

Christaller's Central Place Theory ranks towns according to their services. These include retail shops, professional services and entertainment facilities. Any settlement which possesses one or more of these functions can be termed a **central place**. The rank of the urban area is based on the number and variety of services provided.

For shops and other services to exist, there must be enough demand to produce a profit. Three factors influence the location of different types of shops and services: the frequency of demand for a specific good, the range of the good and the threshold of the good.

Certain goods and services are needed more often than others. Perishable foodstuffs are needed on a day-to-day basis, and these are termed **convenience**, or **lower-order**, goods. Luxuries, clothing and furniture are included in the list of **higher-order**, or **durable**, goods and are bought less frequently.

People are prepared to travel further to obtain higher-order goods, so these goods are described as having a greater **range**. The provision of higher-order goods and services has a higher **threshold**, which is the minimum population needed to provide a sufficient demand for the product. Therefore centres providing higher-order goods are more widely dispersed. More information about services is given on pages 133 – 41.

The location of central places is influenced by population distribution. Where population is fairly evenly spread, a pattern emerges. Each central place serves an area, called its **hinterland**. Lower-order centres have a small hinterland. Several lower-order centres and their hinterlands make up the hinterland of the next-highest order centre, and so on. In theory the hinterlands form a roughly hexagonal shape, although this shape can be distorted by uneven population distribution, communications and physical barriers. According to central place theory, most centres are in the lowest orders. The numbers of centres in each class decrease with ascending order, to only one or two of the highest order.

A survey of particular goods and services available can be undertaken to discover the order of the central place. The hinterland is identified through an analysis of where people travel to for these different goods and services. You may have done this as a fieldwork exercise. If so, look up and revise your results.

The growth and decay of urban areas

Urban areas are subject both to growth and decay.

Growth is the result of:
1 An increase of population by natural means.
2 Migration.
3 Planning.

A town may expand through the setting up of new industries, the development of existing industries, or an increase in services. These activities increase the income of the town, and so often the population increases. This results in a greater demand for services, which provides more employment and attracts further migration, creating an upward spiral.

Although most urban areas in the world are expanding, due to natural population increase, some are contracting. In some parts of the world, traditional heavy industries are declining, partly because of a fall in demand, but also because of competition from products produced in other regions. Urban decay is most likely in towns that have been very dependent on one industry.

In Europe, a number of towns that grew up with the Industrial Revolution are decaying. They have high rates of unemployment, limited ranges of services, inadequate or substandard housing, poor internal communications, and inferior educational and recreational facilities.

Land-use zones

Within a town or city there are different regions based on land use. The pattern of a city's regions is called its **urban morphology**. Most towns and cities have the following regions:

The central business district (CBD)
This is the commercial centre, with the main shopping centre, offices and government departments. The range of shops and offices is related to the rank of the town or city. In small towns, there are various shops selling food, clothes, shoes and furniture. There are also banks and businesses and local government offices. Large towns have department stores, chain stores, shoe and clothing shops, together with shops selling expensive or luxury items like furniture. Regional and national government departments, major banks and finance houses, and head offices are also found. For recreation, there are theatres, concert halls, museums, etc.

Central business districts have the highest rateable values of the city. These values decrease outwards from the **peak-value intersection**, which is the centre where rates and rents are highest. Because the land values are so high, many buildings are several storeys high (called high-rise). Larger cities have secondary business districts located in suburbs.

Residential regions
Most towns and cities have several residential regions (see fig. 4 of chapter 6), with different property prices.
1 Lower price, high-density housing is often found around the city centres and may include older large dwellings and small terraced properties, with high-rise apartments in redeveloped areas.

2 Middle-class residential areas are often suburban, composed of semi-detached buildings.

3 Around the edge of the city are larger, detached properties providing better quality housing. A region of high-class housing is sometimes found near the CBD, with luxury apartments and large houses.

Industrial areas

The industrial regions of a city are found in two principal locations.

1 Older and small-scale industry is found quite near the city centre. Often these industries have declined and the regions are in the process of redevelopment. They may have been replaced by small-scale industry or by warehousing.

2 Modern industrial development is mainly found on the edge of the cities, often along main roads where there are large sites and lower land values.

Twilight zone

This is a region of decaying industry and housing, usually fairly close to the city centre. In some parts of the world, especially North America, the 'downtown' of cities is declining, with competition from out-of-town sites for shopping, recreation and employment. Also, CBDs often 'migrate'. As expansion occurs on one side of a CBD, another part becomes run-down.

It is in these twilight zones that the problems of cities are at their worst, with high crime rates, vandalism, squatting, drugs, homelessness and racial conflict. There is more disease and the mortality rate is higher. Unemployment rates are higher and levels of literacy (reading ability) and of income are below average.

Models of urban morphology

There are several models of urban structure. Figure 3(a) shows the **concentric zone** model. The CBD is at the centre, encircled by the other regions. When there is a river or major communication line, the zones are elongated along it. The **sector model**, fig. 3(b), shows that the regions occur as wedges extending from the CBD along the major routes out of the city. Some people have said that both these models are over-simplified, and that the pattern of regional division is far more complicated. The **multiple nuclei** model, fig. 3(c), recognizes that within a city there are a number of centres surrounded by differing regions.

There is some truth in all three models, although it would be impossible to find a city whose regions exactly matched the pattern of any one of them. In the developing world, other factors have also played a part.

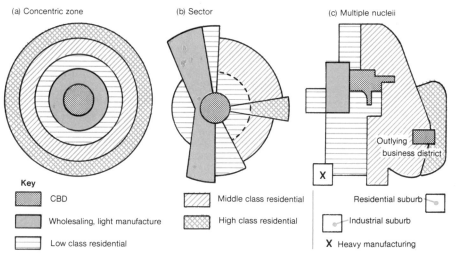

Fig. 3 (a) Concentric zone (b) Sector (c) Multiple nuclei

Social and economic problems

The major problems facing cities include:

1 Housing. Few cities have enough housing. The main housing problems are: insufficient accommodation for the population, too much substandard housing with inadequate services (water supply, sewage disposal, electricity, etc), overcrowding, high property prices and rents.

2 Commuting. People tend to live away from their place of work. Daily travel is by public or private transport. In some areas, the growth of railways, especially underground railways, encouraged commuting and led to the development of suburbs. In the second half of this century, commuting has increased greatly, using buses or private cars.

Commuting has brought problems. During the peak hours when most people travel to and from work, trains become very crowded. The situation is even worse on the roads. Most inner-city road systems are old, with narrow streets and few direct routes. Roads are very heavily used during the peak hours, and long hold-ups occur at junctions. Commuters also have difficulties in parking, because of the shortage of car-parks.

3 Traffic congestion. This is caused by commuters, shoppers and visitors, and by lorries making deliveries or passing through towns

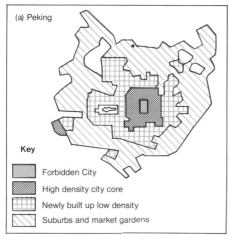

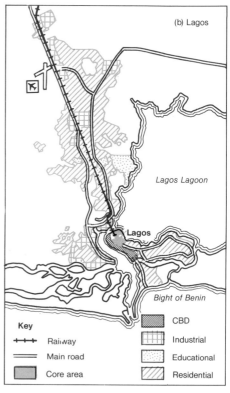

Fig. 4 Two examples of city structure

and cities on their way elsewhere. Many road systems are
inadequate for the volume and scale of modern-day use. Freight
vehicles have become much larger and heavier, causing wear and
tear on the road surface. More road maintenance is required, and
roadworks add to traffic problems. Traffic controls at junctions and
crossroads cause congestion and delays.

4 Pollution. Air pollution is a hazard in all cities. There are several
main sources of pollution, including the burning of fossil fuels and
motor vehicle exhausts (page 62). Another hazard is water pollution
(page 44).

Planning

In order to combat urban problems, local and national governments
have produced various plans.

One way to ease the pressure on major cities is by

decentralization. Restrictions are imposed on development in the existing urban areas and new poles of attraction are set up, encouraging industries and providing housing in areas away from the existing cities.

New towns
In the UK, the New Towns Act was passed in 1946. Fourteen new towns were planned, eight around London. The first were constructed at Welwyn Garden City, Hitchin, Hatfield and Stevenage. Other towns were designated as 'expanded towns', like Basingstoke. Here a small town was chosen to be the nucleus of a much larger town. New road systems were constructed, housing schemes were undertaken

Fig. 5 British new towns

and industries were attracted to the area. There are now 28 new towns in Britain, with a total population of about two million, and over 30 expanded towns. These have taken overspill populations from cities like London, Birmingham, Manchester, Liverpool, Newcastle, and Glasgow.

Other countries also have new towns. In China, plans for the Shanghai city region included provision for 14 satellite towns. The first to be constructed was Minghang, 30 km. from Shanghai, where port facilities could be developed.

Twenty per cent of the French live in Greater Paris. Although suburban developments encircle the city, the central districts (*arrondissements*) remain very crowded. To ease the problems of the city and to control further growth, a master plan was adopted. Five new cities are being built along two axes of development, offering employment in new plants and factories and linked by motorways and express train services.

Developing countries are also attempting to overcome their urban problems. The immense problems of Calcutta are being tackled by the Calcutta Metropolitan Development Authority, which has produced a plan to construct three new urban centres in West Bengal to relieve pressure on Calcutta. Their main difficulty, however, is the lack of capital available for such ambitious schemes. Brasilia, the new capital of Brazil, was planned to encourage growth in the empty interior of Minas Gerais, and to relieve pressure and over-crowding in Rio de Janeiro, the former capital. New communications networks were established, and in 1960, four years after building commenced, the government moved and the new capital was inaugurated.

Green belts
At the same time as new towns were being developed in the UK, planning restrictions were imposed around several major cities. The first restriction was London's green belt, established in 1938. Within the green belt, no further building is permitted except in exceptional circumstances, and the area is maintained as a 'green' area of farmland, forest and recreational facilities (see fig. 5).

Urban renewal
Decentralization is one option. Urban renewal or redevelopment is another. Buildings in the decaying or twilight zones are replaced, where necessary, by purpose-built buildings for housing and employment. New factories are set up and new services and recreational facilities provided.

Redevelopment may also occur in CBDs by replacing older stores with plate-glass, purpose-built shopping facilities, often with covered arcades and on several levels. Examples in London include the Barbican, Covent Garden, the Elephant and Castle, and the reclamation of former docks areas. An example in the centre of Birmingham is the famous Bull Ring development.

In 1978, the Inner Urban Areas Act allowed the institution of **city partnership areas**. Funds were made available from the Government and from the European Regional Fund to help improve inner-city areas. Then in 1980, **enterprise zones** were established to help businesses set up in urban industrial areas, aided by funds and tax and rate-exemptions. The largest such zone is the 320 hectare Salford Trafford Park on the Manchester Ship Canal.

Conservationists are worried, however, that the character of cities is lost through redevelopment, even though many cities are subject to tight planning controls.

Decentralization

Many shopping services, particularly in the USA and France, have become decentralized. France has several types of shopping centre, including city-renewal centres and hypermarket centres. In 1969 there were only 33 planned shopping centres in France, but now there are over 300. The biggest expansion has been of hypermarkets, with at least 50 per cent of shopping centres of this type.

In many cities, the construction of high-rise blocks and the extension of business districts have met the need for more space, but at the cost of increased congestion. One alternative to this is the construction of office parks, spacious new office premises built in suburban areas. One of the largest such schemes is City-Nord, 6 km. north of Hamburg in West Germany, which provides employment for 30,000 people.

Traffic control

One of the major problems of urban areas, already examined, is traffic congestion. In the developed world, there have been many major traffic schemes. Some cities have constructed or extended underground railway systems, or have provided large, free car-parks at out-of-city stations (called 'park and ride' in Britain). The conflict between pedestrian and vehicle usage in city centres has been tackled by a number of **pedestrianization** schemes. Major shopping streets have been made pedestrian precincts, or new pedestrian shopping centres have been built with parking beneath or around the centre. Many cities have multi-storey car-parks, and street parking is banned or restricted by no-parking zones or parking meters.

Attempts have been made to speed up traffic movement in towns, but at great cost. Urban freeways and urban motorways are pedestrian-free, have limited access points and no intersections, therefore traffic can move faster. Often these roads are elevated above the level of existing streets and buildings. Underpasses and overpasses are constructed at junctions. Even with all that has been done, Western cities still suffer a great deal from traffic congestion, particularly at the peak periods.

In the developing world there are fewer urban traffic schemes. Congestion is very bad, although in the poorest countries car ownership levels are very low. The streets of some cities of India and China are very crowded with a combination of buses, cars, lorries, bicycles, rickshaws, carts pulled by mules or oxen, and thousands of pedestrians.

Summary

1 Rural settlement is dispersed or nucleated. Villages may be clustered or linear in shape.
2 The factors affecting the location of settlement include land, water supply, resources, history, communications and industry.
3 Towns can be classified by rank/size or by range of services.
4 The land-use zones of a town include a central business district, residential and industrial areas, and a twilight zone. The three models of urban land use are: concentric zone, sector, and multiple nuclei.
5 Towns and cities experience many problems with housing, traffic and pollution.
6 Planning to improve urban life includes new towns, green belts, urban renewal, decentralization, and traffic control.

Questions

1 (a) Describe briefly how a nucleated village differs from a linear village.
(b) Explain the difference between the terms 'site' and 'location', giving an example you have studied.

(c) Explain the factors that have influenced the development of your example.

2 Choose one British new town and explain three of its distinctive features.

3 For one of the following: Lagos, Rio de Janeiro, Calcutta, Karachi, Dacca:

(a) Describe the features of the city that have developed as a result of its very rapid growth.

(b) Explain how the rapid growth of the city can be considered either as an advantage or as a disadvantage to the whole of the country concerned.

8 Farming

Aims of this chapter

By the end of this chapter you should know about:

1 The farm as a system.
2 The factors affecting commercial and subsistence farming.
3 Examples of different types of farming.

Agriculture can be divided into commercial and subsistence farming.
Commercial farming produces crops for sale, while **subsistence**
farming supplies the needs of the farmer and his family. In most
areas of the developed world there is very little subsistence farming,
except in marginal areas, such as the poorer areas of Italy and
Greece.

The farm as a system

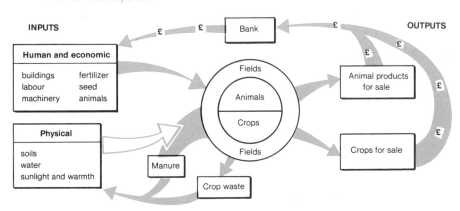

Fig. 1 The farm system

Inputs are what the farmer requires to cultivate his land. The
middle part of the system is the farm itself, which produces the
output. In commercial farming, the output is sold for cash, some of
which is used to pay for the inputs. In subsistence farming, part of

the output becomes the future input, e.g. some of the harvest is kept back for seeds, animal manure is used for fertilizer, etc.

Factors affecting farming

Commercial farming

Commercial farming must be profitable. This depends on supply and demand. **Supply** is the produce that comes from the farm; the **demand** comes from the people who want to buy the produce. The demand for a particular product is known as its 'market'. The farmer tries to supply products for which there is a good market. He wants to obtain the highest quality and quantity (known as the **yield**) possible from his land.

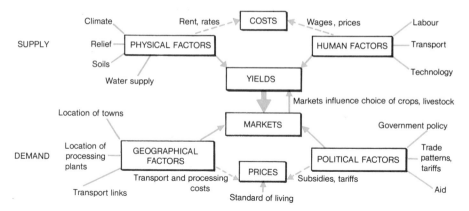

Fig. 2 Factors affecting farming

1 Physical factors: different crops have different temperature and water needs, so farmers select those crops that thrive best in the local climatic conditions. Climate can be modified by the use of heated glasshouses or irrigation schemes, but these are expensive.

Crops are grown more easily on level areas, except river flood plains, which are better suited to pasture. Crops have different soil needs. Wheat and sugar beet grow best in rich, fairly heavy loams, while barley is more suited to lighter, drier soils. Heavy clays are used for pasture, and light sandy soils for market gardening. Thin and acid soils are usually left as natural pasture, suitable only for sheep and goats. Soils can be improved by deep ploughing, fertilizers

and by adding minerals, e.g. reducing the acidity of some soils by
adding lime.

2　Human factors. In the developed world, agricultural labour is
scarce because wages are low and working conditions hard. This has
encouraged mechanization. Arable farming requires less labour than
mixed farming and dairying. Market gardening needs the most
labour, but only at certain times of the year, so casual seasonal
labour is employed.

The level of technology is quite important. Modern methods of
cultivation make more efficient use of land. Careful seed-selection
helps to increase yields, and soil analysis allows the most suitable
fertilizers to be selected for the type of soil.

The use of fertilizers is quite expensive, and capital is required to
buy farm machines. However, these costs are often lower in the long
run than the cost of labour. Improvements in transport, so that
products can be moved quickly and, where necessary, in refrigerated
containers, have widened the markets for farmers.

3　Geographical factors. The type of market depends on the size of
the population centre (or centres) being supplied, the level of income
and the tastes of the population. Communications are a very
important factor because they extend or limit the farmer's market
and the cost of transport has to be added to the cost of production.
One of the cheapest ways of transporting in bulk is by water, but this
is also the slowest means of transport, whereas air transport is the
fastest but also the most expensive. So grain is mainly transported
by boat, but perishable fruits are carried by lorry or aircraft. Thus
communications affect the size of markets in three ways:
availability, cost and speed.

4　Political factors. The main impact of government agricultural
policy is on prices. Subsidies can be given to farmers to keep prices
low, and customs duties can be levied on imports, making them more
expensive. Governments also influence farming by tax incentives,
grants, reclamation and improvement schemes, and education. In
Europe, the Common Agricultural Policy of the EEC has made
available considerable funds to assist farmers.

Factors affecting subsistence farming
Subsistence farmers cultivate their land to provide food and clothing
for their families. Any surplus can be sold for cash or bartered for
goods the farmers cannot produce themselves. The main factors are
climate, relief, soils and level of technology. Within these limits, the
farmer will produce those crops with the greatest yields and which
will provide as far as possible what his family needs.

Types of farming

Scale

K Commercial farming can be extensive or intensive. **Extensive** farms
are large, while **intensive** farms are small and have higher yields
per hectare. Small farms are often labour intensive which means
that they use a lot of labour in production. Machinery is generally
more important on the large farms, replacing labour in cultivation.
Extensive farming involves the large-scale production of cereals, and
the rearing of livestock, notably beef cattle and sheep. Intensive
farming is generally related to the production of specialized crops,
like fruit and vegetables, and the keeping of dairy cattle, pigs and
chickens.

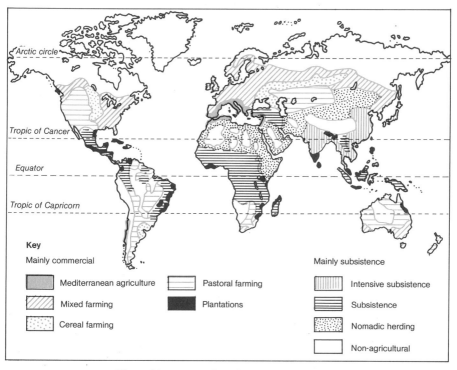

Fig. 3 Major agricultural regions of the world

Land tenure or ownership

There are different forms of land tenure. The main division is
between owner-occupied farms and tenant farms. Farmers who own

their own land are more likely to invest in improvements. Short leases on rented holdings can have a bad effect, because tenant farmers are reluctant to invest in the land because the benefits will be experienced only in the long run.

Crops

Monoculture is the cultivation of only one crop, or rearing of one type of livestock, while **polyculture** means that there is more than one crop or type of livestock. Monoculture can be financially risky, because a poor harvest brings great hardship to the farmer. Polyculture is often more successful. Rotation of crops maintains the fertility of the soil with less fertilizer, and the cultivation of a range of crops insures against too great a financial loss.

Types

arable	cereals or root crops
market gardening	fruit or vegetables, usually on a smaller scale than arable farming
horticulture	flowers
viticulture	vines
pastoral farming	livestock
mixed farming	livestock and crops

Fig. 4 Types of farming

Products	Location	Size	Other features
Market gardening			
Vegetables, salad stuff, soft fruits, bush fruits.	Around large towns; warm areas with light soils.	Small, <10 ha.	Labour intensive. Fast transport to urban areas, freezing or canning plants.
Orchards			
Apples, pears, plums, peaches, citrus fruits, bananas, etc.	Cool temperate, warm temperate, tropical.	Small, 10 ha. to 30 ha.	Casual labour for harvesting. Fast transport to urban areas or canning plants.
Vine growing (viticulture)			
Wine, sultanas, currants.	Warm temperate, Mediterranean climates	Small to medium	Labour intensive, becoming more mechanized.

Table continues

Products	Location	Size	Other features
Arable farming			
Cereals, e.g. wheat, barley maize. Roots, e.g. sugar beet, potatoes. Vegetables.	Temperate continental interiors of N America, E Europe, central Asia.	Large (from 60 ha. to 30 000 ha.)	Mainly mechanized. Crops to flour mills, sugar refineries, or fodder for livestock.
Mixed farming with dairying			
Cereals, root crops, vegetables, cattle, pigs.	Cool temperate moist areas: NW Europe, SE Australia, New Zealand.	Small (10 ha.) to medium (800 ha.)	Mixed labour/ machines. Fodder for livestock, milk fresh or for butter, cheese, etc.
Mixed farming with stock raising			
Beef cattle, fodder crops	Temperate areas: upland valleys for breeding, lowlands for fattening.	Medium to large (3000 ha.)	Low labour needs. Transport of beef by refrigerated container, or 'on the hoof'.
Sheep farming			
Hay for fodder, sheep	Poorer upland or arid regions. Lambs from hill farms fattened on lowlands.	Mainly medium to large	Low labour needs. Sheep supply lamb, mutton, wool.
Mediterranean agriculture			
Traditional: wheat, olives, sheep.	Remoter parts, uplands.	Very small.	Labour intensive. Little mechanization.
Irrigated: fruit, vines, vegetables.	Valleys, coasts, tourist areas.	Small to medium.	Labour intensive.
Rice farming			
Rice, vegetables.	Warm, humid, or warm with water supply: SE Asia	Small	Land irrigated. Fragmented holdings. Labour intensive, little mechanization.
Plantation agriculture			
Coffee, tea, bananas, oil, palm, rubber, sugar cane.	Tropical or sub-tropical areas, lowland and hillside.	Very large (up to 4000 ha.)	High labour needs. Mechanized. Cash crops, exported to Europe, N America.

Fig. 5 Types of farming in the major agricultural regions

Wine production in France

The vine is the most important crop in France. It prefers a summer temperature of at least 20°C, and so cultivation is concentrated south of the Loire valley. French wines are world-famous and are produced in the most favoured localities (see fig. 6). Champagne comes from the northern limit of wine growing, and the small rather acidic grape produced gives champagne its distinctive flavour. Other areas produce an inferior wine, known as **vin ordinaire**.

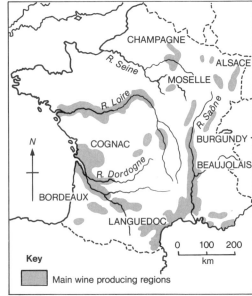

Fig. 6 Wine production in France

Market gardening in California

The Central Valley of California is bordered by the high Sierra Nevada to the east, and the Coast Range to the west. The valley has low and gentle relief, with deep alluvial soils and a Mediterranean climate. The Shasta, Folsom and Friant dams provide irrigation water, which is channelled through canals. Farms are small, 30 to 40 hectares, but are highly mechanized, and packaging and marketing are modern and efficient. The Delta area, where salad crops and vegetables are grown, is the main region for **truck farming** (market gardening). Elsewhere, tree crops are important, especially citrus fruits, peaches and vines.

Arable farming in North America

There are several regions devoted to different crops in North America (see fig. 7). In the corn belt, maize is the principal crop, grown principally for feeding livestock, in rotation with soya beans, wheat and hay, on farms averaging 70 to 80 hectares.

Because the Prairies have cold winters, wheat is sown in spring and harvested in early autumn. The spring wheat region extends from the Dakotas to the foothills of the Rockies, with a flat landscape of large rectangular fields and straight roads. Cultivation is highly mechanized on the large farms, which average 500 hectares, so there is a small workforce, but these extensive methods of cultivation result only in fairly low yields. The climate gives enough warmth and sunshine in the short summers for the wheat to ripen, and usually rainfall is adequate, while the rich black soils are ideal for wheat cultivation. Usually there are large surpluses for export, but even here, crop diversification is occurring, to balance poor years.

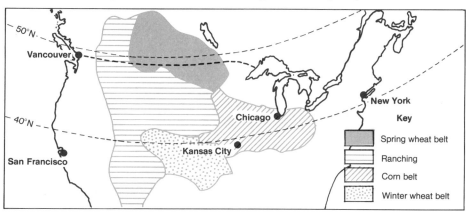

Fig. 7 Crop belts in North America

Collective farming in the USSR

The Soviet Steppes, extending eastwards from the Ukraine to the heart of Asia, are similar to the Prairies. Extensive wheat farming is aided by level land, rich soils, and a continental climate, but towards the east and south, lower rainfall results in the use of dry farming techniques, and yields are often low. Farming is organized by the state, and the land is divided into vast state farms (*sovkhozi*) and smaller collective farms (*kolkhozi*). The *sovkhozi* are over 30 000 hectares and are run by the state, while the *kolkhozi* average 6000 hectares and are run on a cooperative basis. The *kolkhozi* are mainly mixed farms with wheat, sugar-beet, fodder crops and market gardens, while the *soukhozi* concentrate on large-scale wheat cultivation.

Farming in East Anglia and the Fens

East Anglia is composed of a low plateau covered with glacial deposits, and the Fens are made up of silt and peat deposits. The Fens were marshland until drainage commenced in the seventeenth century, transforming the area into the most productive farming region of the UK. This has not been without problems; many parts are now below sea level due to shrinkage (caused by peat drying out). A complex system of dykes, embankments and pumps assist drainage and protect the land from flooding.

Over 50 per cent of the land in East Anglia is arable, producing wheat and barley in rotation with sugar beet, potatoes and field vegetables, on farms of about 200 hectares. Eighty per cent of the Fens is arable, growing similar crops, with the addition of market gardening, soft fruit cultivation around Wisbech, and bulbs and flowers around Spalding. Methods are intensive and yields are high.

The region has many advantages for arable farming. Physical advantages include warm summers (21°C), sunshine and low rainfall (less than 650 mm.), a variety of soils, many of them fertile, and flat or undulating land suited to large-scale mechanized farming. Economic advantages include the accessibility of London and Midland markets, modern techniques with high investment in irrigation, machinery, etc., specialization permitting efficient methods, and contract farming, e.g. field vegetables for frozen-food companies.

Dairying in Europe

In many areas, dairying is very efficient and highly organized. Breeding is carefully controlled, producing animals with high milk-yields. More farmers now breed multi-purpose animals, providing meat as well as dairy products. Milking is mechanized, and there are efficient collection, processing and marketing facilities, e.g. creameries in Ireland, cooperatives in Denmark and Sweden. Pasture is kept at a high standard by reseeding, grass management and strip grazing. In regions like South-West Ireland, little extra feeding is required. However, in countries like Denmark, winter feeding is essential for survival. In Scandinavia and Switzerland, **transhumance** is practised. The lower land of the valleys is devoted to the production of fodder crops. Cows are pastured on the higher slopes in summer, and stall-fed throughout the winter. On parts of the North Italian Plain, cattle are factory-farmed. They are stall-fed throughout the year, while the land is used to produce fodder crops.

As urban populations have grown and transport has improved, the demand for liquid milk has greatly increased. Areas with poor communications and regions with a particular specialism continue to provide the dairy products of butter, cheese, cream and dried milk. Often, creameries provide liquid milk, but use any surplus for butter or dried milk. In a number of regions, dairying is carried on in association with pig-rearing and fattening, for the skimmed milk provides a useful food for pigs.

Ranching in the USA

In the western USA, the rainfall is too low and erratic for cereal production, so the area is left as grassland. Vast areas are needed for the large herds of cattle, because the grass is poor. Wind pumps lift water for the stock. Cattle are kept on ranches which are highly organized for stock breeding and rearing. Land is divided by post and wire fences, and grazing is carefully controlled. Cattle are normally sent to the corn belt for fattening, but increased irrigation in the dry grasslands means that more fodder crops are being produced and more cattle fattened on the ranches.

Cattle rearing in the savanna

On the tropical grasslands rainfall is scanty and erratic, and the grass is of poor quality, but temperatures are high. This results in disease and faster evaporation of surface water. In Africa, cattle herding is associated with subsistence farming. Many of the tribes in countries like Uganda, Kenya and Tanzania cultivate sorghum and maize. Cattle graze over a wide area, and tribesmen herd them to different pastures through the dry season. The main breed of cattle is the Zebu, which is a hardy animal. Hides are exported from the northern savanna lands, but elsewhere the cattle are kept for meat and as a measure of wealth.

Sheep farming

Most sheep farms in Europe are hill farms. The small areas of better land are used for hay and vegetables, while the sheep roam freely on the hills and moorlands (see page 71). Most sheep are kept for wool, and the harsher conditions produce a better fleece, with thicker and longer wool. The production of mutton has declined greatly, but there has been an increase in the output of fat lamb. Like beef cattle, the lambs are often bred in poorer areas and then transported to the richer grasslands of the lowlands for fattening. Overall, the number of sheep has decreased, because the profit margin in sheep farming is often insufficient to give farmers a standard of living which compares with other occupations. Also, there is considerable competition for land in upland areas, sheep having to compete with forestry, the building of reservoirs, and recreation. Under the Common Agricultural Policy, many agricultural regions where sheep are most common, are reducing production, and other employment is being provided.

Farming in the Mezzogiorno

The *Mezzogiorno* covers two-fifths of Italy and contains over eighteen million people. It has many problems, including a poor natural environment, a lack of resources, and an unsettled history. Less than 12 per cent of the region has flat land suitable for cultivation. Most is steep, requiring terraces, and soils are poor and thin, and much eroded. The climate causes problems, for although the high temperatures and sunny weather are good for crops, the summer drought affects the water supply. In the upland areas, wheat is cultivated using dry-farming techniques. Land is left fallow in alternate years, for the soils are not rich enough and there is not enough moisture in them to cultivate the land every year. Yields are low. On the slopes, and on the drier parts of the uplands, olive trees are grown, for they can withstand both drought and infertile soils. On the stony uplands, sheep and goats graze as best they can, providing wool, meat and milk. Beside the farms are small patches for cultivating vegetables for the family, and there may be some vines as well. Holdings tend to be small and fragmented.

In the coastal areas and in upland basins, citrus fruits are most important. Vineyards are found wherever there is water available for irrigation, and quality wines are produced. Vegetables are very important, especially around Naples.

The traditional landscape of the *Mezzogiorno* is being transformed. The first major step was taken in 1950, when the *Cassa per il Mezzogiorno* (the fund for the South) was established. Four problems were identified: **1** land tenure, so land reform was essential; **2** shortage of water in the drought, so irrigation schemes needed improvement; **3** the shortage of productive land, so reclamation was needed; **4** the unwillingness of farmers to change their methods, so education had to be improved.

Land reform started in 1950 with the redistribution of land from large estates to small farmers and labourers. Fifteen years later, 700 000 hectares had been allocated to 100 000 households.

The largest irrigation scheme involved the construction of the Apulian aqueduct. Water is carried from the headwaters of the Sele in Campania, across the Apennines, and supplies about two million

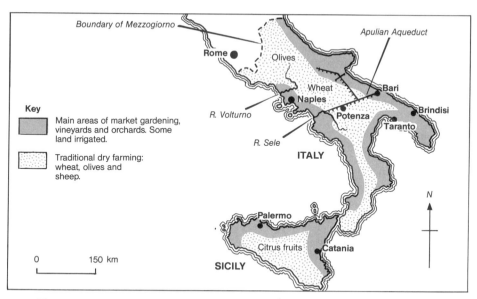

Fig. 8 Farming in the *Mezzogiorno*

people. Three reservoirs and five dams have been built in the Sila valley.

The swamps and badly drained areas around the coast have been reclaimed. In Calabria, the plain of Sant' Eufemia has been reclaimed, with new villages, roads and irrigation networks, so that it is now intensively farmed.

Rice farming

Rice is the stable crop of most of South-East Asia, and of half the world's population. Its cultivation allows a large population to survive at subsistence level. Lowland rice is grown mainly in padi fields, embanked and flooded to supply the water the crop requires; most rice-growing areas require irrigation systems to provide adequate water supplies. Rice cultivation is described on page 70.

Coffee in Brazil

Coffee is cultivated mainly on *fazendas*, large estates, situated on the eastern edge of the Brazilian Plateau where rich *terra rossa* soils, summer temperatures over 20°C and a well-distributed rainfall provide suitable conditions for coffee. There have been many problems: falls in coffee prices in years of over-production, and disease, and soil exhaustion. Gradually the system is being changed to avoid over-dependence on one crop, and to restore fertility to the soil. More food crops, oranges, cotton, and sugar cane are now grown. Some areas are being used as pasture for fattening beef cattle.

Rubber in Malaysia
Rubber plantations are many hundred hectares in extent and are found in Western Malaysia at heights below 300 metres with an equatorial climate. This is because the rubber tree requires uniform temperatures over 25°C and at least 1800 mm. annually of well-distributed rainfall. Rubber is native to Amazonia, but seeds were smuggled out and plantations established in South-East Asia. Plantations require a lot of capital and good transport and marketing, because rubber is mainly exported to the developed world. Scientific management is necessary to ensure that high yields from the rubber trees are maintained, and also for the initial processing of the latex before it is exported.

Shifting cultivation
This is practised in parts of the humid tropics. Small plots of land are cleared, then cultivated for two or three years. They are then abandoned as the soil loses fertility, and the process is repeated elsewhere. It is often termed 'slash and burn'. This method is still found in equatorial forest regions, particularly in Amazonia, Indonesia, West Africa and the Philippines. (See Amazonia, page 72.)

Nomadism
This is a subsistence form of pastoralism found in dry regions, where livestock are moved periodically in search of pastures. It has declined in recent times.Over-grazing has caused desertification, and many of the nomads have died of starvation or migrated to more favoured regions. The main region of nomadic herding is the Sahel of northern Africa, and parts of central and eastern Africa.

The Sahel is the belt of semi-arid grassland to the south of the Sahara desert, and has been experiencing drought since 1968. Tribes like the Tuareg herded cattle, sheep, goats and camels from one area to another as pastures became exhausted. Initially the drought resulted in the loss of over half the cattle, but since 1980 there has also been massive loss of human life, due to starvation and disease. Despite extensive aid programmes, the situation will remain critical for many years to come.

Summary

1 Commercial farmers produce crops to sell, subsistence farmers produce products for their families.
2 The farm is a system with inputs and outputs.
3 Physical factors that influence farming include climate, relief, drainage, and soils.
4 Human factors that influence farming include labour, technology, markets, communications, and government aid.
5 Intensive farms are small, with high yields per hectare. Extensive farms are large, often highly mechanized, and the productivity of the land is low.
6 Farming can be divided into market gardening, arable, pastoral and mixed farming.

Questions

1 (a) Name one type of crop farming that is intensive. Give a located example.
(b) Which type of commercial farming is most extensive? Give a located example.
(c) What is the difference between monoculture and polyculture?
2 For any one type of farming that you have studied:
(a) Draw a diagram showing the farm as a system.
(b) List three inputs and three outputs.
(c) Describe the physical factors that have influenced the type of farming.
3 For a contrasting region, explain how economic factors have affected the type of farming.

9 Resources for industry

Aims of this chapter

By the end of this chapter you should know about:

1 The factory as a system.
2 The factors affecting the location of industry.
3 Sources of raw materials.
4 Sources of power, coal, oil, and natural gas, and nuclear and hydroelectric power production.

What is industry?

Farming, forestry, fishing, mining and quarrying are called **primary industries**, because they produce or extract basic materials. Most of the products require processing before they are used.

Industries like food processing, metal smelting, mineral refining, chemical processing, and manufacture are known as **secondary industries**, because they process the products of primary industry.

Shops, finance, administration, transport and tourism are **tertiary industries**, because they serve or depend on primary and secondary industry.

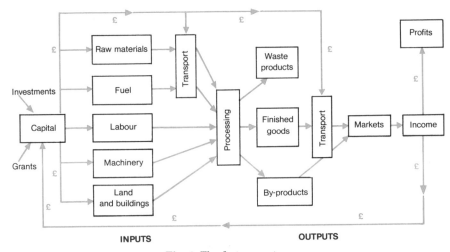

Fig. 1 The factory system

The factory as a system

Like farms, factories are units of production in a system, as fig. 1 shows. The inputs are influenced by a number of factors. These govern the location of the industry.

Factors affecting the location of industry

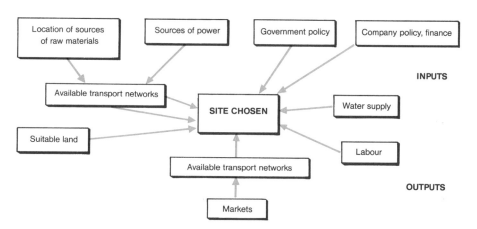

Fig. 2 The factors affecting the location of industry

Raw materials
Industry processes materials. The input may be in its 'raw' state, like iron ore for the steel industry. Other industries use materials that have already been processed, e.g. steel sheets for the motor car industry.

Power
All modern industries require power; some use electricity as their main source of power. Industries are often sited close to a cheap source of power. Coal, oil and natural gas are used as fuels. Whether a factory is situated closer to the source of power, or to the source of the main raw material, depends on the cost of transport.

Government and company policy
These can affect industry in several ways. Some industries are encouraged to have factories in areas of unemployment because of government help. Industrial development in other areas can be

discouraged by conservation laws. These measures occur at national level, but are increasingly influenced by international policy.

Multi-national groups are firms that have companies in many countries of the world. A large industrial corporation can choose from sites in many parts of the world. Locations can be affected by mergers, by takeovers and by changes in company policy.

Land and water
In selecting the actual site for a plant or a factory, land and water supply are important. Level land is needed for building on, and for very large plants, cheaper land is desirable.

Many industries need a water supply. Some of this may be cheaper coming from a river or the sea than from the piped water supply. Whichever site is chosen needs to have adequate services, communications and labour supply.

Labour
In the past, location was often affected by the cost of labour. An area with cheap and plentiful labour attracted industries. This is no longer so significant in the developed world, because of standard national wage rates. If necessary, workers can be attracted to an area by high wage rates or attractive environments and working conditions.

Markets
Small-scale industry is more affected by the need to be near its market than are the huge companies that operate on an international scale. Firms producing items like clothing are often found near or in large cities. On the other hand, large electrical or chemical firms are supplying products on a much bigger scale. Good communications are far more important to them than the distance from large urban areas.

Transport
The aim of industrialists is to find a factory or plant location somewhere between the sources of raw materials and the markets, so that transport costs are at their minimum. If an industry uses several raw materials, factories are sited close to the source of material required in greatest quantity or heaviest in bulk. This is one reason why so many industries were sited on the coalfields. It was cheaper to transport the other raw materials than the fuel.

Location is affected by the transport available. Heavy goods can be transported quite cheaply, if slowly, by water. Where there are canals, waterways or sea routes, goods can be carried long distances. This affects the location of plants processing imported raw materials. The most suitable sites are often at the point of entry of materials into a country, which is why many heavy industries are located at ports.

The most expensive part of transport is the transfer of goods. **Transfer costs** are due to the use of machinery and labour in loading and unloading goods between different forms of transport. This has been partly overcome by technological advances, e.g. the use of container ships and the construction of container ports. Cranes can simply lift loaded containers from boats directly on to lorries or railway trucks, and vice versa.

The type of transport used for a product is related to the product's value per unit of weight. Iron ore is of low value compared with its weight, so that transport costs make up a high proportion of the total cost. Small, high value items, like jewellery or electronic devices, are light, and the cost of their transport comprises a very low percentage of their total cost.

Other points to note
The cost of each individual item falls as production increases. This is termed **economy of scale** and occurs because often the same amount of machinery is required regardless of the amount produced. Also, special discounts are available for buying and transporting goods in bulk. The term given to the production of goods on a very large scale is **mass production**.

Finally, a very important element in explaining the present-day distribution of industry is **geographical inertia**. This is when an industry remains in an area, although the factors that governed the choice of the site are no longer important. Such is the case with textile industries which developed using local supplies of wool, but now import the wool or produce other fabrics.

There are two main reasons why factories remain on these sites:

1 Because there has been a great deal of investment in plant and machinery at the site. Adapting, expanding and replacing various parts of the plant are cheaper than starting again from the beginning.

2 The existence of an industry leads to the development of a skilled labour force, suitable transport facilities, and a pattern of marketing. Together these can make it worth while for the industry to remain on the original site.

Raw materials

Iron ore

Iron has been mined for many centuries, originally on a very small scale. Charcoal was used to smelt the iron. The introduction of coking coal to the process led to great expansion, mainly in the areas where iron working was already taking place. From 1860 onwards, Bessemer converters were used to make steel.

Iron ore seams vary from small thin outcrops, now mainly exhausted, to thick extensive seams with large reserves. The iron content of the ore varies from about 25 per cent to 60 per cent. Mining takes place by both shaft and open-cast methods. Shaft mines extend downwards to the seams, and the iron is then removed horizontally along the seam from each side of the shaft. Where the seams are at the surface, open-cast mining occurs, and huge excavators remove the iron, leaving large quarries. With the latter method, seams do not need to be so productive because costs are lower.

In Minnesota, iron ore is mined in the Mesabi Range, by open cast methods. The overlying glacial drift is removed and enormous open-cast pits are dug, e.g. Hull Rust mine is 4 km. long and over 100 m. deep. The iron ore is taken by rail to the ports of Lake Superior, then by boat to Lakes Michigan and Erie. It is smelted at Chicago, Cleveland and Buffalo, or taken by rail to Pittsburgh. Annual output is about 100 million tonnes. The higher-grade ores are running out, so lower-grade ores are now being exploited.

Other metals

Other mineral resources include copper, lead, zinc, tin, bauxite, silver and gold. Most minerals are found in igneous and metamorphic rocks.

Chile is the world's largest producer of copper. There is a giant open-cast mine at Chuquicamata, 3 km. long and 300 metres deep. 100 000 tonnes are extracted daily, and there are reserves to last another hundred years. The ore is transported by rail to the port of Antofagasta and almost all is exported, although there are several smelters in the region and at Santiago.

Chemicals

Potash, salt, sulphur and mercury are among the chemicals mined. In some places, salt and potash are not mined but removed by open-cast methods or by pumping. Water is poured down shafts into the salt deposits, then the brine pumped out and the water content evaporated.

The main use of these substances is in the chemical industry. Potash is important in the production of fertilizers, salt for sodium compounds, and sulphur for acids and other products. The chemicals produced then provide the basis for pharmaceuticals, cosmetics and chemicals needed in the processing of other products.

Quarrying
Quarrying occurs in many upland areas. Granite and sandstone are quarried for building materials, and in the past, slate was quarried for roofing. Some types of hard limestone and marble are used in construction.

Other materials are also extracted from the ground, including sands and gravels used for road-making and construction. Often the most useful sources of supply are fluvioglacial deposits in lowland areas. Fine sands are used in the making of glass, and in several areas where these are found, glass-making is an important industry. Feldspar is one of the minerals of which granite is composed, and weathering can convert it to kaolin, china clay. Deposits of kaolin are quarried for use in the pottery industry, especially in the making of china.

Outcrops of chalk and limestone are quarried. They contain calcium carbonate, which is the raw material for cement production. Cement works mainly grew up either close to the source of supply, or where the raw material could be transported by water. Sometimes, however, a cement works has continued to function after the original source of supply has been exhausted. This is an example of geographical inertia.

Forestry
Thirty-three per cent of the world is covered by forest. There are three main types:
1 **Broad-leaved evergreen forest**, in tropical regions, e.g. Amazonia (see page 72).
2 **Deciduous forest**, which occurs in temperate maritime regions.
3 **Coniferous forest**. Large areas of Scandinavia, the USSR and Canada still retain their natural forest cover. Areas of marginal land, especially heathland and moorland, have been re-afforested. Lumbering is a carefully organized activity. There is careful selection of trees to be cut, conservation, and replanting. This is very important, because many of the most accessible areas of forest have been over-exploited, and it takes a long time for new trees to grow to maturity.

Large-sale timber industries are found in Scandinavia. Most saw and pulp-mills are situated near the mouths of rivers, especially in

Sweden, and are powered by hydroelectricity. The main use of woodpulp is in the production of paper for newsprint, but other types of paper are also produced, and chemicals extracted for the making of rayon, wood alcohol and resins.

Sources of power

Coal

From the Industrial Revolution until the 1950s, coal was the main fuel for heating, smelting, and the production of steam power. The easy availability of coal was an important factor in the growth of the industry in Europe during the last century.

Many coal seams are not exploited, either because they are too thin and faulted, or because they are already worked out. For coal mining to continue, the cost of production has to be less than the price paid for coal. Demand for coal has fallen, while the cost of extracting coal,

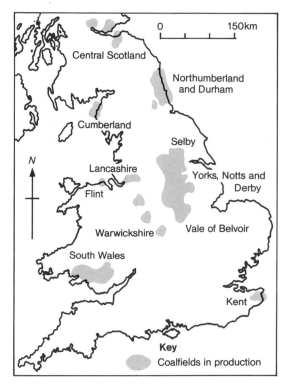

Fig. 3
Coalfields in the UK

especially for equipment and labour, has continued to rise. Now, only the accessible and most productive seams can be worked economically.

Most coal is extracted by shaft mining. Once the coal has been brought to the surface by conveyor belts, it is transported by rail, or by barge where waterways are available.

Coal mining in South Wales expanded rapidly until 1913, when there were 630 mines and production reached its peak. Coal was exported through the ports of Cardiff, Barry and Swansea, or was used in the iron and steel, copper and tin-plating industries. As demand for coal and steel fell, unemployment rose and the region became very depressed, economically.

Government aid led to the establishment of industrial estates like Treforest, and the siting of government departments like the motor tax office at Swansea. Some of the old industrial areas, like the Lower Swansea valley, have been reclaimed. However, unemployment remains very high, over 40 per cent in the old mining villages, and the environment does not attract new industry. Only two iron and steel works, and one tin-plating works, remain. The coal industry

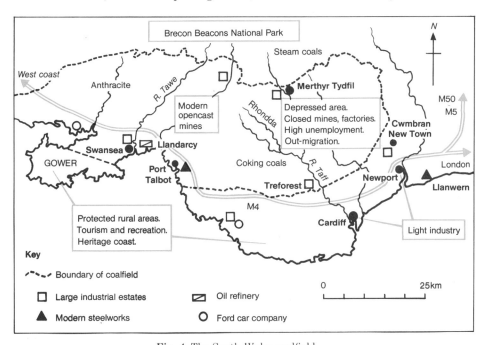

Fig. 4 The South Wales coalfield

continues to contract, with more pits closed every year, and now is concentrated on the mining of anthracite in the west.

Oil

The use of oil has increased very rapidly since the Second World War. Huge reserves of oil were discovered in developing countries. These were exploited by Western companies which extracted the oil and transported it to Europe at a price much lower than coal. There has been a considerable change in recent years, and oil is now an expensive fuel, partly because resources have diminished, but mainly because the oil-producing countries set up OPEC (Organization of Petroleum Exporting Countries) to safeguard their interests and to ensure a high price for the product.

Oil is refined to produce a range of products, from heavy diesel fuel to the lighter petroleum used by road vehicles. Oil contains many chemicals, and the by-products of oil refining support a huge petrochemical industry. From these chemicals, synthetic fibres and rubber, fertilizers, pharmaceuticals and many other products are manufactured.

Oil is transported by huge oil tankers to terminals from which it is piped to refineries. In the past, oil refineries were mainly situated on the coast. Now, with the development of a network of pipelines, they are located in many areas. Once the oil enters the refinery it is piped to fractionation towers where the oil is heated and distilled. Heavier oils are piped off from the lower levels, and lighter oils from the higher levels. The products are then stored for transport by road tanker, or passed directly into the products pipelines.

Gas

Gas comes from two sources: 'natural gas' from gas fields located in sedimentary strata, and 'town gas' manufactured from coal. Manufactured gas was piped to homes for heating and cooking. Gas is used less in industry than coal, oil and electricity as a fuel or power source, but it is a useful raw material for the chemical industry because it contains many of the chemicals also found in oil. The main products are ethylene, used in anaesthetics; glycol, for anti-freeze; acetone, which is used in the production of synthetic fibres; and many other hydrocarbons.

One of the most significant developments in the geography of natural gas was the discovery of the North Sea gasfields. Then in 1970 the first major oilfield, Forties, was discovered. The UK is now self-sufficient in oil, but the reserves may only last another 10 years. Oil rigs and platforms at the fields extract the gas and oil, which are then transported by underwater pipes to terminals around the coast of Britain and continental Europe.

Electricity

1 Thermal power. Electricity can be generated from coal or oil. The fuel is burnt to heat water and convert it into steam, which is channelled to turn turbines. These turbines cause dynamos to rotate, producing an electric current, which is carried by transmission lines to the consumers.

Coal-fired power stations are found on the coalfields and near large towns and cities, providing electricity for their populations. As population has increased, the greater demand for electricity has been met by building more power stations, but the newer stations tend to use oil rather than coal.

2 Water The force of water was in the past used to turn a water-wheel, which in turn operated a piece of machinery, e.g. turning a millstone to grind corn. Water is now used in the generation of electric power, and fig. 5 shows how. HEP (hydroelectric power) production occurs in upland regions where valleys can be dammed to create artificial lakes; and along rivers in lowland areas. Barrages built for flood control, navigation or irrigation, can also be utilized for HEP production.

In 1962 the Akosombo dam was constructed across the Volta River to create the huge Lake Volta. This led to the development of a new inland fisheries industry, helped transport by developing lake ports, and in the north provided water for irrigation. However, the main reason for the project was to provide electricity. Most of the money for the development came as loans, mainly from the USA in return for permission to exploit bauxite deposits and to build an aluminium

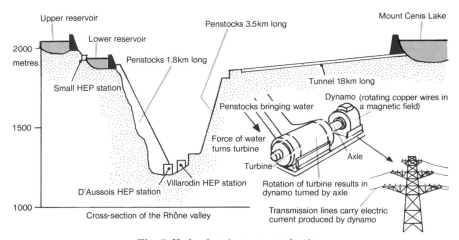

Fig. 5 Hydroelectric power production

refinery at Tema. The electricity is used in the aluminium industry and is transmitted to the main towns of southern Ghana.

Although the project has brought some advantages, there have also been problems. Over 80 000 people had to be resettled, causing many social and economic problems. Less industry than expected was attracted by supplies of cheap electricity and there is still a large loan to repay with high interest rates.

3 Nuclear power. There has been great growth in this form of generation. Little raw material is required, it does not rely on fossil fuels, and unlike HEP production, it is not tied to particular locations.

Uranium rods are fed into a reactor, where a chain reaction splits the atoms. The heat given off by this reaction heats gas which converts water to steam. The steam is used in the same way as in thermal power stations. The steam then passes to cooling towers, where it returns to a liquid state and is re-used.

Most nuclear power stations are located in areas with limited power resources. In some countries, governments have fostered the development of nuclear power, e.g. France has encouraged the nuclear power industry, with its first nuclear power station built in 1956 near Avignon. Today 40 per cent of France's power is generated by nuclear power stations.

It is perhaps surprising that there are not more nuclear power stations, but there are serious disadvantages. One is the very high cost of installation. The other is the risk of radioactivity, for the waste from the reactor is radioactive and therefore disposal is difficult and potentially dangerous. In Britain there is a strong anti-nuclear campaign based on safety and conservation of the environment.

Thermal power station	_Oil terminal_	_Oil refinery_	_HEP station_	_Nuclear power station_
Location				
Near large towns or industries, or on coal or oilfields	Coast: ria or estuary	Away from major urban centres	In mountains or on rivers	Away from urban areas because of risk of explosions, radioactive leaks

Table continues

Thermal power station	Oil terminal	Oil refinery	HEP station	Nuclear power station
Raw materials				
Coal, oil	Crude oil	Crude oil	Water	Uranium
Land				
Large flat site	Protection for ships from storms	Large flat site	Valleys that can be dammed	Large flat site
Water				
Supply for cooling	Deep water channel for large tankers	Plentiful supply for cooling	Regular supply, not limited by freeze or drought	Supply for cooling
Transport				
Water, rail, road or pipe-line. Transmission lines.	Tankers to bring oil, pipeline to distribute it.	Pipelines Road tankers	By transmission lines	

Labour and capital
Only a small, skilled workforce required. All these plants are capital intensive.

Example

Lynemouth		Milford Haven	Volta River	Chinon

Fig. 6 Site requirements

Summary

1 Industry is divided into primary, secondary and tertiary.
2 The factory is a system with inputs and outputs.
3 Factors that affect industry include raw materials, power, site, labour, transport, markets and government policy.
4 Raw materials come from farming, fishing and forestry, or are mined or quarried.
5 Electricity is produced in thermal power stations using oil or coal, or from water or nuclear power.

Questions

1 (a) What fuel is normally used in a nuclear power station?
(b) State two advantages and two disadvantages of nuclear power production.
(c) Suggest two main requirements for selecting a site for a new nuclear power station.
(d) Imagine you are leading a protest group against the proposed siting of a nuclear power station close to your home. Suggest three reasons you would put forward to a government enquiry to support your case.

2 (a) Name one coalfield in a developed country which has suffered a severe decline in output in recent years and state three factors which have led to this decline.
(b) Suggest three ways in which the economy of a depressed coalfield region can be improved.

3 (a) Explain what is meant by the terms 'primary industry' and 'tertiary industry'.
(b) What is 'geographical inertia'? Give a named example.

Aims of this chapter

By the end of this chapter you should know about:

1 Traditional and modern industrial regions.
2 Links between industries.
3 Examples of different types of industry.

Industrial regions

Figure 1 shows how important primary industry is to the developing world. Secondary industry is more important in the developed world, and tertiary industry is most important in the developed countries. As countries develop, they become less dependent on primary industry, and the tertiary sector grows.

Traditional industrial regions
These are based on heavy industry, often located on coalfields and engaged in metal smelting, heavy engineering, chemical manufacture or textile production. These industries are now known as **smokestack** industries. Traditional industrial regions can be recognized by:
1 A high proportion of employment in manufacturing industry.
2 The existence of industries like those listed above.
3 High-density housing, often of inferior type, and poor services.
4 An unattractive environment, e.g. pollution, waste tips, etc.
5 Problems caused by closure of factories because of a world-wide fall in demand for these products, resulting in unemployment, areas of derelict land and emigration.

The Ruhr coalfield, West Germany
This is a good example of a traditional region. It is one of the major industrial regions of Europe, covering an area of about 11,700 sq. km., with a population of eight million people. Coal and steel formed the basis of the economy, but as the demand for coal has declined, so the industry has contracted.
    The iron and steel industry developed in the Sieg valley using local iron ore with charcoal for smelting. Charcoal was replaced by coking coal from the Ruhr valley. Even after the iron ore was exhausted, the industry remained, using imported ore brought by waterway to the

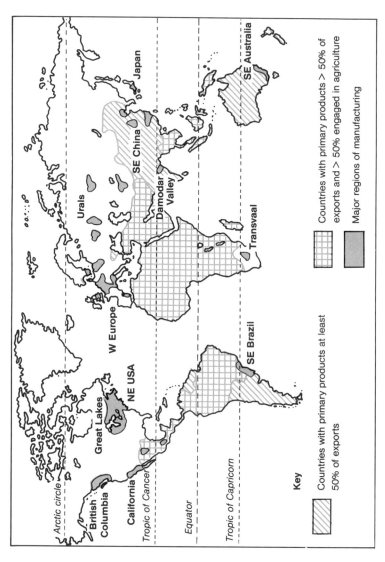

Fig. 1 Primary industry and industrial regions

Ruhr. Formerly, every major city had important iron and steel works. Only Gelsenkirchen and Hattingen remain important in the central Ruhr, and all but two of Dortmund's plants have closed. Blast furnaces are concentrated in the western Ruhr, which saves transport costs.

Modern technology has contributed to the shift in location. Sintering (mixing iron ore and coke) takes place at Europoort (Rotterdam), blast furnaces are becoming larger and more efficient, and electric oxygen steel converters have been introduced. The Ruhr region is responsible for 80 per cent of West Germany's total steel production.

What can be done to help traditional industrial regions? The Ruhr Regional Plan has attempted to tackle the problems of the Ruhr. Changes in the industrial structure have led to the decay of some areas, and there are problems of industrial waste and pollution. In the plan, urban development is concentrated along seven north-south spines which contain the five major cities of the region: Duisburg, Essen, Gelsenkirchen, Bochum and Dortmund. Between these spines are buffer green belt zones, where recreational opportunities have been increased. New transport links improve accessibility between the centres. The aim is to make the region more attractive to people and new industries.

The future prosperity of the Ruhr will be based less on the products of coal and steel, for which it became famous, and more on the new industries like the huge Opel assembly plant at Bochum, and new chemical plants. Universities, out-of-town shopping centres and new parks are appearing, to produce a 'New Ruhr' landscape.

Clydeside
Glasgow, Scotland's largest city, grew up on the River Clyde as a market town which expanded into a port dealing with American trade. Port industries developed, associated with the import of tobacco, sugar and cotton. The Industrial Revolution brought large-scale industry to the area, using coal and iron ore from the Lanarkshire coalfield. The production of steel supplied heavy-engineering industries, like the manufacture of railway engines and textile machinery. However, the most important industry to develop was shipbuilding. At one time, 30 km. of riverside were lined with shipyards, producing one-third of British ships, including the *Queen Elizabeth* and the *QE2*.

The region's major industries have declined rapidly since the Second World War, due to falling demand for products and competition from more favoured locations elsewhere, in England and overseas. The port has moved from Glasgow to Greenock, but there has been no large-scale industrial development. There are few modern growth industries, but some stimulus has come from the North Sea oil developments providing contracts in the shipyards for oil rigs and platforms.

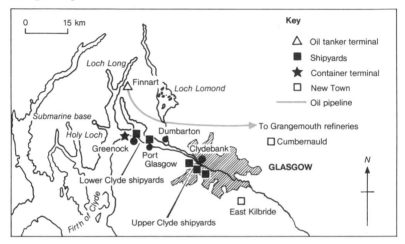

Fig. 2 Clydeside

Glasgow has experienced many problems. Migration from the rural areas of Scotland and Ireland caused severe overcrowding and poor living conditions. Unemployment increased as factories closed down and the port declined. Clydeside is now a special development area, receiving government grants. The inner city region is being redeveloped. The tenements have been replaced by high-rise blocks and open spaces, local transport has been improved, and industrial estates have been built. However, only 40 per cent of the former population could be rehoused in inner Glasgow, so the remainder have moved to new housing estates in the outer suburbs, or further afield to Scotland's five new towns.

Ways of helping depressed industrial regions
1 Improving services, especially road networks.
2 Reclaiming derelict land.
3 Improving the quality of housing available, building attractive shopping centres, and increasing recreational facilities.
4 Providing more open spaces.
5 Building industrial estates.
6 Giving special grants and concessions to attract modern industry.

Industrial estates
An industrial estate is a planned industrial development. It is sited where there are good communications, especially by road, away from residential areas. On the estate, roads link standard factory units of different sizes available for rent, and sites are offered for purpose-built units designed by individual companies. The estate provides services like banks and public houses, and usually has plenty of car-parking and good bus services to the residential areas.

Modern industrial regions
These areas of light industry are often found in or around population centres. They produce consumer goods, with an emphasis on electrical and electronic production. These industries are often called **sunrise industries**. This name comes from 'Silicon Valley', so named because it is the centre of computer technology using silicon chips. Silicon Valley is in California, where people can enjoy a good climate and work in very attractive surroundings. Sunrise industries can be recognized by:

1 Modern, pleasant factories, well-spaced in landscaped surroundings.

2 Excellent communications, with wide roads serving the factories, close to motorway intersections, and often close to airports.

3 The industries use modern technology and produce high value goods per unit of weight, many of them for the consumer market.

4 Some of the jobs command great skill and high rates, but many require little training and are mainly routine.

High technology in southern England
The western corridor along the M4 has been named 'Silicon Valley' because, like its counterpart in California, it has many growth industries based on the use of the silicon microchip. The M4 provides easy access to London, to Heathrow airport, and there is a good Inter-City railway service. A mainly rural environment provides attractive living and working conditions. Swindon and Reading are the main growth towns of the region. Swindon was formerly important as a railway town, but now it has widened its industrial base and attracts new industries because of communications, sites available on industrial estates, plenty of housing, and low rates.

   Although most new industry is linked to the computer revolution, other industries have developed, supplying the needs of the computer firms, e.g. service industries, precision engineering, banks and insurance centres. The future of the new industries depends on research and initiative, producing new ideas ahead of rivals in Japan, Taiwan, South Korea, Singapore and Hong Kong.

Links between industries

In industrial regions, groupings of industries are common. The existence of raw materials or particular industries attracts other industries. Concentrations develop for a variety of reasons, through links between the different companies. There are several types of linkage. One of the most common occurs when different firms are engaged in stages of the production of a product (see fig. 3).

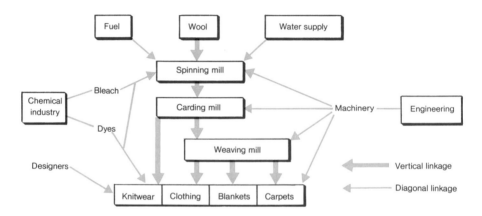

Fig. 3 Linkage in the textile industry

Where several different industries occur in the same region because they have similar location requirements, they are said to be in association. Examples include the coalfield industries, which all need a lot of coal, or port industries which are all dependent on imported raw materials. Location leaders are large firms that set off a chain-reaction by attracting further industries to serve them or to make use of their products. A chemical complex is a good example of a location leader. Dependent industries are locationally tied to a major industry because they use its products, for instance companies in the petrochemical industry use the by-products of oil refining.

   Footloose industries are those industries which are not tied to particular locations or to associations of industries. Development regions try particularly to attract footloose industries, because they can easily be sited in depressed or deprived areas.

Types of industry

Requirements for selected industries

Iron and steel	Motor cars	Electrical and electronic
Raw materials		
Iron ore, limestone	Cheap steel, mechanical components	Small amounts of refined metals, plastics. Parts.
Power		
Coking coal, or cheap electricity for electric furnaces	Plentiful electricity	Electricity
Site		
Large level site. Water supply for cooling	Large level site. Car assembly plants are very extensive	Good services, as on industrial estates
Labour		
Large labour force	Large labour force	Links with research laboratories
Transport		
Good network – water or rail for raw materials; road and rail for products	Focus of road network – for assembling many components, and transporting products	Good road communications
Markets		
Steel-using industry, e.g. ships, aircraft, machine tools, vehicles, domestic appliances.	Efficient system of advertising and marketing, with many retail outlets	Modern industries, wholesale and retail outlets
Examples		
Ruhr	European	S England
Damodar valley	German	California
Teesside	Midlands	Clydeside
Clydeside	Japan	Japan

Fig. 4 Requirements for iron and steel, car and electrical and electronic industries.

Textiles	Chemicals
Raw materials	
Natural fibres: wool, flax, cotton. Synthetic fibres – oil by-products, rayon	Coal, oil, natural gas, salt, sulphur, potash, limestone, nitrogen, vegetable oil, wood
Power	
Coal/electricity	Plentiful electricity
Site	
Adequate space, good water supply – textile manufacture, hosiery, knitwear, etc. – industrial estates. Clothing firms – mainly city locations	Large level site, good water supply, isolated – if making dangerous chemicals
Labour	
Skilled labour force. Capital intensive for synthetic fibres. Labour – intensive for clothing	Small labour supply but some highly trained chemists. Capital intensive
Transport	
Near ports for imported materials. Good access to population centres	Water, road or rail for bulk commodities. Good transport to markets
Markets	
Fabrics to clothing, furnishing firms. Finished goods to shops, etc.	Pharmaceutical & cosmetic firms, industries requiring chemicals for processing.
Examples	
Teesside	Teesside

Fig. 5 Requirements for textile and chemical industries

Regional case studies

1 Iron and steel in the Damodar valley, India: the valley of the River Damodar, a tributary of the Hooghly, contains India's most important coalfields. Some of the coal is used for thermal power production, e.g. at Bokaro, and coking coal forms the basis of an iron and steel industry. Iron ore is mined close by, and limestone is also available. These materials are transported by rail to a number of steelworks, (see fig. 6). Steel is then exported by road and railway to Calcutta.

Dams have been constructed across the River Damodar to provide hydroelectric power for industry and irrigation water for the Burdwan area, which now supplies the industrial towns with food.

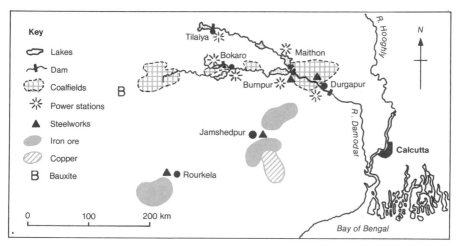

Fig. 6 Industry in the Damodar Valley

2 Motor car manufacture in Europe: motor car manufacture is one of the biggest industries in the world. Japan and the USA are the major producers, but several European countries are important, especially West Germany, France, Italy, Spain and Britain.

Most larger car-assembly plants in Europe are found close to major cities. The main reasons for this include: the good communications links available, the large labour force available, and the big local market, for the greatest demand for cars originates from large cities.

While West Germany, France, Italy and Spain have expanding car industries, motor manufacture has been through a period of decline in Britain, partly because of overseas competition. The main centre in Britain is the West Midlands, focused on Birmingham and Coventry. The industry grew up here because precision engineering was a major industry, providing a skilled labour force, and the area's central position aided the transport of component parts to the plants. Excellent communications allowed the export of cars to the main conurbations and overseas via Liverpool, Southampton and London, and finally there were plenty of large sites available for car assembly plants.

3 Engineering and chemicals on Teesside: coal from the Northumberland and Durham coalfield formed the basis of industrial development in North-East England. Much was exported, while the remainder was used in the local iron and steel industry, smelting iron ore from the Cleveland Hills. Steel supplied the shipyards of the

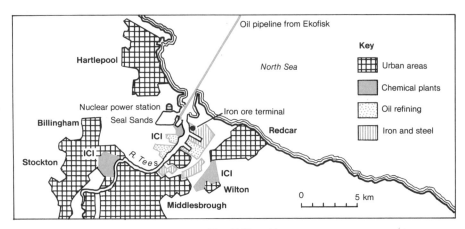

Fig. 7 Teesside

Tyne and Wear and heavy engineering works on Tyneside and Teesside. All these industries have declined and there is high unemployment, much derelict land, and some areas still have poor housing and social conditions.

The main growth industry is chemicals, Teesside having the largest concentration of chemical plants in the UK. Large oil refineries distil crude oil for the chemical plants. Potash comes from nearby Eskdale, and at Billingham, fertilizers, chlorine and sodium are produced. The most important chemical plant is ICI at Wilton, covering about 550 hectares and employing 10 000 people. It produces a wide range of oil-based chemical products, including many synthetic fibres like nylon, polyester and terylene. Forty per cent of the products are exported to EEC countries.

The North-East is designated as a development region. The Team Valley industrial estate on Tyneside employs 20 000 people, and there are many other smaller estates. There are three new towns, and urban redevelopment schemes are underway in cities like Newcastle upon Tyne, replacing substandard housing with modern developments, and improving communications.

4 The European electrical and electronic industry: the electrical and electronics industry is one of the fastest-growing sectors of the European economy, increasing by about 10 per cent per year. The industry is dominated by American companies, but there are several very large European companies as well, e.g. Philips, centred on Eindhoven in the Netherlands, and Siemens, centred on Munich in West Germany.

Products range from large machinery for use in power stations, telephone exchange systems, systems controlling railway and underground railway traffic, to innumerable small household items like fires, lights, radios and televisions. Electronic products are becoming increasingly complex and more widely used: the most rapidly growing branch is computers. At the top end of the market are missiles and space satellites.

5 The industrial development of Japan: Japan, the USA and West Germany are the premier industrial nations. Japan has few natural resources, importing half its coking coal, iron ore, textiles and mineral oil. However, it has many major industries, including cars, shipbuilding, engineering, electronics, chemicals, plastics and textiles.

The growth of industry is the result of:

(a) Government aid, including heavy subsidies.

(b) A large labour force. In the past, wage rates were low, so Japanese products were sold at a lower price than their American and European rivals, and this established new markets.

(c) There are plentiful supplies of HEP.

(d) Japan has good communications to its densely populated neighbours in the Far East.

(e) Most production is controlled by large corporations, e.g. Sanyo, Sony, Nissan, etc., which use efficient and sophisticated technology, modern management techniques and aggressive selling policies.

The four main industrial regions occur in densely populated areas providing labour, with locations permitting the use of sheltered ports, rivers and HEP.

Summary

1 Traditional industrial regions are declining, but high tech sunrise industries are expanding.
2 Many industries cluster together, because they are linked in various ways.
3 Footloose industries are not tied to particular sites.
4 Most traditional industries require a large supply of raw materials, power and labour, but modern industries are mainly capital intensive and need little raw material.

Questions

1 Look at fig. 1.

(a) Name three countries with large exports of primary products, and three countries with important industrial regions.

(b) Choose one industrial region. List its main industries. Describe the factors that have aided the development of industry in that region.

2 (a) Give an example of a traditional and a high tech industry.

(b) Explain why many traditional industries are declining.

3 (a) What is a 'footloose' industry?

(b) Give an example of a footloose industry you have studied.

(c) Describe its location and give two reasons for the choice of that site.

(d) What are the main features of a modern industrial estate?

Aims of this chapter

By the end of this chapter you should know about:

1 The types and location of service industries.
2 The factors affecting transport.
3 The factors affecting tourism.

As manufacturing industry develops and people's living standards rise, the demand for services increases. In the USA, 68 per cent of the working population is employed in the tertiary sector, and many countries in Europe have over 60 per cent. This contrasts with countries like the USSR (41 per cent) and developing countries like Malawi and Ethiopia, with less than 10 per cent.

Services occur at many different levels, as the table in fig. 1 shows. Some are geared to industry, some to people, but many services are used by both industry and people, e.g. roads and railways. Low-order services, e.g. hairdressers, are more common and widespread than high order or more specialized ones like accountants. There is a hierarchy of services (see page 84). Some services are organized on a national level but are available almost everywhere, especially those that supply direct to the consumer, e.g. electricity, water supply, postal service.

National	Regional	Local
Government and administration		
	1 *For population*	
Seat of government. Civil Service	County law courts	Town halls
	2 *For industry*	
Dept. of Trade & Industry	Regional Development Corporations	Factory offices
Public services		
	1 *For population*	
Electricity supply	Hospitals	Schools
	2 *For industry*	
Telephone systems	Postal sorting offices	Waste disposal

Table continues

National	Regional	Local
Transport		
	1 *For population*	
Inter-City rail	Coaches	Buses
	2 *For industry*	
Freight trains	Road haulage	Local deliveries
Finance		
	1 *For population*	
Credit card companies	Personal loan companies	Building society branch offices
	2 *For industry*	
Stock market	Insurance companies	Branch banks
Marketing and research		
Advertising firms	Research institutions	Showrooms
Personal services		
Ombudsman	Barristers	Hairdressers
Retailers		
Mail-order firms	Department stores	Corner shop
Recreation		
Television	Theatres	Public Houses

Fig. 1 Types of services

Location of services

Most services are found near their customers. A threshold of demand is required, that is, a minimum number of people who will purchase a service. Several factors influence locations:

Communications and access
The customers of a local food shop are within walking distance, but a hypermarket needs a good road system linking it with the population. However, both need good communications for supplies. Cinemas and theatres tend to be in the centre of towns and cities, so that people from a wide area can travel to them.

Administration is often centralized in head offices in major population centres. Most large cities have a quarter which houses most of the major offices and business enterprises (e.g. the City of London). Banks, insurance firms, finance houses, marketing firms, and administrative offices are usually found close to one another.

Labour
Labour is important, because tertiary industries are often very labour intensive. The unit of the industry is the employee, not the product, because it is people's skills that are being purchased. Large

city locations have the advantage of being able to draw on a large pool of labour.

Markets
The market depends on the threshold of the service. A much smaller population is required to support a grocery shop than a department store. Everyone needs to buy food often, but fewer and less frequent purchases are made at a department store.

The markets for industrial services are factories and plants, so their location is an important element. National services tend to cluster together. Other services are often found close to the point of production, e.g. transport firms, local banks, industrial cleaners.

Land
Sometimes land is the most important factor of location, e.g. hypermarkets need a large area, away from the high land prices and congestion of city centres. Land is also important for recreational services, particularly sports complexes and golf courses.

Clustering
Agglomeration is the way in which groups of services tend to cluster together. Town centres have a great range of shops, and often several shops selling similar goods. Shops grouped together tend to attract more customers. From this, special areas develop in cities, e.g. the Champs-Elysées, Paris and Fifth Avenue, New York for fashions.

Transport

Although transport employs only a small number of people, less than 7 per cent in Britain, most economic activities depend on it. Transport distance can be measured in three ways: **1** actual distance in kilometres; **2** time distance, based on the length of time taken to travel a route; **3** cost distance, based on the expense of travelling a route. In selecting the means of transport, either time or cost will be the determining factor.

Networks and accessibility
As communications develop, they begin to link places together to form a network. Networks are made up of nodes and links. A **node**, or **vertex**, is the meeting point of two routes, a point of origin, a point of destination or any sizeable town along a route. Every road that joins two nodes is called a **link**, or **edge**. These are shown on a topological diagram as straight lines connecting the nodes (fig. 2). As you can see, it presents a simple version of the road system, ignoring minor deviations. Developed networks have many links, which

means that places are well connected. Networks can be measured in two ways:

1 by dividing the number of edges by the number of vertices. The result is an **index of connectivity**;

2 by adding up the number of edges that converge on each vertex. The result is an **index of accessibility**. The vertices can then be ranked in order of accessibility.

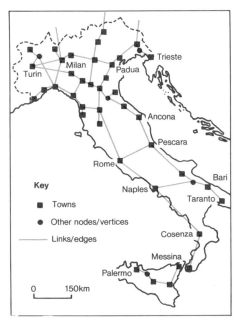

Fig. 2 Italian motorways

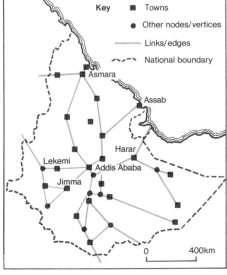

Fig. 3 Ethiopian roads

Factors affecting communications

1 Demand. The demand for communications is influenced by the size of population. The greater the population, the greater is the demand for transport. People require supplies of food and manufactured products, so transport links are necessary between the points of supply and the places where people are living, and between the sources of raw materials and the places of manufacture. In summary, the existence of communications depends on:

1. The number of people living in an area.
2. Their demands based on income, travel to work, links with other places.
3. The transport of food supplies and manufactured goods to people.
4. The movement of raw materials.
5. Tourism and recreation.

Sparsely populated regions have less-developed networks, because demand is lower. The main exception is in regions which are rich in raw materials, when there are transport facilities to take the raw materials to the markets.

There are **through**-routes and **link**-routes. Link-routes connect adjoining settlements or sources of supply with sources of demand. Through-routes link places that are more widely separated, ignoring intervening places.

2 Routes. The actual siting of routes is influenced by the following:

1. The location of cities, towns, villages, industry and raw materials.
2. The pattern of trade between them.
3. The nature of the landscape between them.
4. The type of climate experienced.
5. The money available for overcoming obstacles.

Few natural barriers cannot be overcome, but it is cheaper to build roads and railways on land that is level, firm and well-drained. The most expensive aspects of route building are the construction of bridges and viaducts and the excavation of tunnels. Because of this, routes tend to follow the easier ways, even if they are longer; i.e. skirting mountain ranges, following valleys, Expensive routes are taken only when essential, e.g. in Switzerland and Austria, or to aid development, e.g. the Panamerican and Transamazonian highways in South America.

There are many smaller problems that increase the cost of construction. In areas liable to flooding, routes have to be raised above the flood level. Urban areas may have to be avoided, or roads and railways raised above the level of the buildings unless there is large-scale demolition.

Climate has a number of effects. In mountain areas and regions of heavy snowfall, snow needs to be cleared from roads and railways. Gritting and salting are required to prevent icy roads and frozen points. On mountain sides, it is often necessary to have protection from avalanches and snow drifts. Torrential rains can cause landslips in areas of steep slopes, either blocking or washing away communication lines. Fog is a hazard both for airports and for motorways.

Routes tend to avoid areas with these climatic problems. However, this is often impossible, because of local needs. Therefore a lot of money is invested in snow-moving equipment for road, rail and runway clearing, and ice-breakers for ports. Some motorways and runways have under-surface heating to keep them free of ice.

Tourism

K

Tourism is an important sector of tertiary employment. Many people are employed in the provision of accommodation, meals, entertainment and transport for tourists. Tourism fosters the growth of retailing, of construction industries, and of craft industries providing souvenirs. In some regions, employment is seasonal because the holiday season is limited by the weather, but other areas attract visitors throughout the year.

Tourist regions

There are several types of tourist region. The most popular is the coastal region. The coasts around the Mediterranean are the most visited holiday region in the world. Other types include winter sports regions, found mainly in mountainous areas, and scenic tourist regions. These are very scattered and include a great variety of landscapes. Towns also attract tourists, because of their historic monuments and their cultural facilities.

Factors affecting tourism

1 Demand. Since the last century, the demand for holidays has increased rapidly. There are several reasons for this. In the developed world, improvements in the standard of living, and an increase in leisure time, permit many more people to have holidays. Television and advertising persuade people that they want to take holidays and visit places.

2 Communications. The opening-up of tourist areas has been aided by improvements in transport. Travel is easier by car, with better road systems and motorways. More important in recent years has been the expansion in air transport. For example, air travel allows the British to travel anywhere in Europe in less than four hours' flying-time from London. The advent of package holidays has reduced the cost of air transport. Package holiday operators plan holidays on a large scale. They charter aircraft and reserve accommodation in bulk, so reducing the price per head. In order to do this, they need a large number of purchasers of holidays, so massive advertising campaigns are undertaken.

3 Attractions. There are several different features that favour the growth of tourism:

1. Climate. Most people expect to have warm, sunny weather for beach holidays. This is one of the main reasons for the importance of tourism in southern Europe. The Mediterranean climate offers almost consistently high temperatures, long hours of sunshine and low rainfall through the peak holiday season. People taking winter holidays have specific climatic requirements, either higher temperatures than home, or snow suitable for skiing.

2. Landscape. Many people like to spend their holidays in an attractive environment, which often means mountains, lakes, spectacular sea coasts; landscapes that have not been completely altered by man.

3. History and arts. The history of an area plays an important part in its potential attractiveness. People visit ancient or picturesque towns and archaeological sites, and enjoy exploring castles, palaces and churches.

4. Economy and culture. Two other factors that can play an important part in enticing tourists are life-style and price. Many tourists like to observe local customs, enjoy different food dishes, and different entertainments. Apart from that, if a region provides for the needs of tourists cheaply, it is likely to become very popular.

Benidorm, Spain
The Costa Brava, the Costa Blanca and the Costa del Sol are the main Spanish regions for tourists. The original fishing and farming villages have grown out of all recognition. The coasts now present a scene of closely packed high-rise hotels and apartments. These regions have become popular with holidaymakers from more northerly countries, owing to the combination of good weather, attractive scenery and low prices.

The resort of Benidorm is a typical result of the tourist boom. It grew up as a fishing village which by 1960 had a population of 2500, on a low headland between two sheltered bays. It possesses seven kilometres of clean sandy beach, low humidity and high temperatures, and is only two hours' flying time from major urban centres in North-West Europe.

Benidorm is now the largest holiday resort in Spain, offering over 250 000 beds in hotels alone. The growth has occurred through investment by businessmen from Valencia, by local people and by the tour operators. Over 20 000 people live there, but the migrant staff are not allowed to live in the town.

The main amenities offered in the town are accommodation – in older and smaller hotels, newer multi-storey block hotels and apartments; shopping within the major area in the old town, but with newer centres around the hotels; and entertainment – barbecues, night clubs, discos, etc.

Although tourism is a valuable source of revenue to the Spanish, it produces many problems. In 1977 a law was passed to control the supply of tourist services in the popular and congested areas, and to plan developments for regions with a tourist potential. Minimum standards were laid down. All tourist areas must have a supply of drinking water, sewage treatment, electric power, communications and car-parks. Other controls have been introduced to protect the natural environment.

Invisible exports

Tourism is an invisible export, being a service rather than a product that is bought. Foreign tourists are encouraged by countries that need to earn more foreign income. A number of developing countries have tourist industries, e.g. Gambia and the islands of the Caribbean. Tourism helps local employment and industry, as well as providing valuable foreign currency to purchase imports with.

Improving facilities for tourists is considered to be a good way of helping deprived regions, because it stimulates the local economy and provides jobs. The EEC provides financial assistance for schemes to improve communications, services and recreation facilities, to aid tourism in Europe's problem regions.

Other services can earn foreign income as well. Banking, finance, insurance and professional services in Britain provide invisible exports which help the country's trading position.

Summary

1 Activities that provide services are termed tertiary industry. This occurs at different scales: local, regional and national.
2 The location of services is influenced by communications, labour, markets and land.

3 Communications form networks that can be measured. Transport is affected by demand and the physical environment.
4 Tourism is affected by demand, communications and attractions like climate, landscape, history and economy.
5 Invisible exports earn foreign currency when services are bought by foreign countries. Tourism is an important invisible export.

Questions

1 (a) In what part of London is most office employment located?
(b) State two features of the area where most employment is located.
(c) State three reasons why most office employment is located in that area.
(d) Why are most city offices in tower blocks?
2 (a) State two difficulties arising from office employment in cities.
(b) Because of the difficulties, many offices have moved to new locations. Name one office complex you have studied which has moved to a new location. Describe the new location and explain why it was chosen.
3 (a) Look back to fig. 2. Name the most accessible place on the network in Italy, and give a reason for your choice.
(b) What is a transport network?
(c) Compare fig. 2 with fig. 3. Which network has the better connectivity? Explain your answer.
(d) Although car travel is more costly than train travel in its use of energy, people in Britain make twenty times as many journeys each year by car as by train. Give two reasons which help to explain this fact.

12 Development and trade

Aims of this chapter

By the end of this chapter you should know about:

1 The measures of development.
2 The poverty cycle.
3 Increasing food production and improving resources.
4 Trade and aid.

Developed and developing nations

Measures of development
Development is measured by calculating the GNP (Gross National Product). This is the total value of a country's home and foreign output, and indicates its economic wealth. There is a broad division between the developed world and the developing world.

The development gap
The great contrasts between developed and developing nations are termed the **development gap**.

	Developed world	*Developing world*
Birth rate per 1000	less than 20	over 30
Life expectancy	over 70 years	less than 50 years
Population growth	less than 2%	over 2%
Literacy	over 80%	mainly less than 40%
Food consumption (calories)	over 3000	less than 2500
Agriculture	Commercial	Subsistence
Employment: Primary	Less than 5%	over 50%
Secondary	30–45%	15–40%
Tertiary	50–65%	10–20%
GNP	High	Low

Fig. 1 The development gap

The developed countries include the main industrial nations. Developing countries have some wealth and industry, but these are very unevenly distributed and large areas have primitive methods of production. Developing countries are also very vulnerable to natural and economic disasters. Drought and floods bring famine and starvation, and weak economies are badly affected by trade recessions.

K ▶ *The poverty cycle*
Poverty is one of the main results of underdevelopment. It creates a vicious circle (see fig. 2) which is very hard to break.

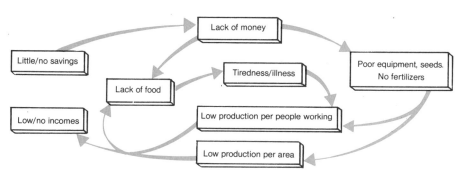

Fig. 2 The poverty cycle

Reasons for contrasts in development
In the developing world, development is hampered by:
1 The lack of modern industry.
2 The lack of capital.
3 The lack of technology and an industrial base.
4 Traditional farming techniques.
5 Over-population.
6 Cultural and religious conservatism or taboos.
7 Low standards of education.

Some of the problems of development are associated with relations with the developed world.
1 Developing countries have borrowed massive amounts of money from developed countries, which they cannot afford to repay. Often these loans were given at high rates of interest, so many countries are crippled by having to find money for interest repayments.
2 Trading patterns favour the developed world. Primary products, the main exports of the developing world, have a lower value than

the manufactured goods developing countries need to import. Also, developed countries sometimes have trade barriers to protect their home markets from imports of lower-priced manufactured goods.
3 Developing countries provide a major market for armaments. Their willingness to incur expenditure on defence and on wars increases their debts to the developed world.

Food production

Food shortages

Food shortages occur wherever food production does not meet the population's needs and there is too little income from other economic activities to purchase food from elsewhere. Two-thirds of the world's population suffers from a shortage of food. People are under-nourished if they do not have enough food, or malnourished if they do not have enough variety of food. At least 400 million people live on the brink of starvation.

Insufficient food production is the result of:
1 Poor farming techniques, resulting in low yields, inefficient use of land, soil exhaustion and soil erosion.
2 Shortage of cultivated land, mainly due to lack of adequate water supplies.
3 Natural disasters, like drought, floods and typhoons.
4 Large fertile areas used for cash crops such as coffee, tea, sugar, tobacco and cocoa for export, rather than for food crops for local populations.
5 High birth rates and rapid population increase – more mouths to feed from the same amount of land.

Food surpluses

While the developing world cannot feed itself, there are large production surpluses in the developed world. Governments subsidize farmers in Europe and North America to ensure adequate food supplies. The result is a surplus of food production. In North America, the main surplus is of grain; in Europe of dairy products, fruit and wine.

Reasons for surpluses include:
1 Large areas of highly productive land.
2 Skilled land management, with high yields aided by seed selection, fertilizing, soil conservation, a high level of mechanization, careful stock breeding and feeding.
3 Small populations compared to the agricultural output.

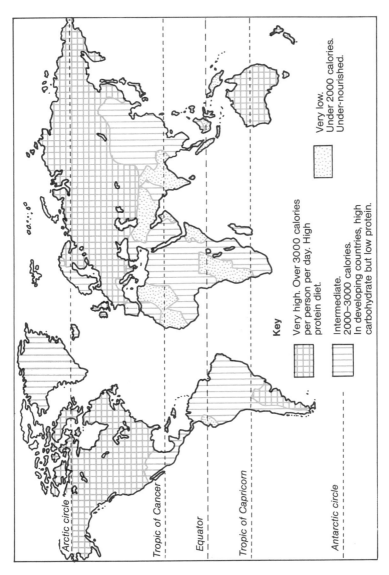

Fig. 3 World food consumption

These surpluses are not exported to developing countries short of food, because:

1 Food prices are high in Europe and North America, and transport over long distances would make the food even more expensive.

2 Many of the developing countries cannot afford to import food, because they are already greatly in debt to the developed world.

3 Even when food is imported from the West, distribution is hampered by poor communications in the interior regions away from coasts and rivers.

Food surpluses can be supplied as part of aid programmes, but when this occurs there are often strings attached, e.g. the provision of grain by the USA in return for political support. The EEC will not consider exporting surpluses as part of an aid programme because it is said to be too expensive.

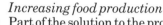

Increasing food production

Part of the solution to the problem of world hunger is to increase food production. Most land suited to agriculture is already cultivated. The main way of increasing food supplies is by improving land and methods of production, so that yields are higher. Yields can be increased by irrigation, by biological control of pests, improving seeds and careful breeding, and by fertilization.

1 Irrigation

See Aswan Dam (page 44), Volta River Project (page 117).

2 Soil management

Soil fertility can be improved. Crop rotation aids fertility, because different crops use different minerals from the soil. Therefore root crops can be grown to replace the nitrogen removed by cereal crops. Alternating land between crop growing and pasture also helps.

Fertilizers improve soil fertility. Animal manure is a simple and effective fertilizer, but in many areas dung is dried to be used for fuel, instead of being spread over the land. Artificial fertilizers are made from chemicals, e.g. potash, or from oil by-products. Although effective, they are expensive and usually need to be imported. They can have bad side-effects by polluting water supplies and upsetting the ecological balance.

Soil erosion can be reduced by keeping a protective vegetation cover during seasons of high wind or heavy rainfall. This prevents soil being blown or washed away. Contour ploughing, ploughing along the lie of the land, or terracing reduces the amount of soil washed away from sloping land.

3 Technology

The use of machinery can increase food production. Mechanical ploughs can turn over the soil to a deeper level, and break up hard pans (a cemented layer of soil below the surface, occurring in many regions of heavy rainfall, that hinders drainage). Mechanical harvesting and threshing can reduce wastage.

Pesticides and insecticides can destroy pests and insects that attack crops. Swarms of locusts can consume entire crops in minutes. They are most common in a belt stretching from North Africa across the Middle East. The most effective way of dealing with them is by spraying the swarms from the air.

Disadvantages to the use of pesticides and insecticides include the cost. Also, insects become immune, so the quantity of chemicals has to be increased. Destroying pests and insects can upset the balance of the ecosystem, leading to further problems. Chemical pollution of soils and water can result.

In the 1960s, a programme of improving farming in the developing world began. It became known as the Green Revolution. The use of modern technology, fertilizers and seed selection was intended to revolutionize food production in the hungry world. Scientists produced hardier, high-yield plant strains, e.g. Mexipak, a wheat strain developed in Mexico that trebled wheat yields, IR-8, a rice strain developed in the Philippines that more than trebled rice yields. However, IR-8 was very prone to disease, so newer varieties have been introduced that are both high-yielding and disease resistant, e.g. IR-22 which is now grown widely in India, Bangladesh and Vietnam.

In addition to seed selection, it was hoped that production would be increased by extending irrigation, by application of fertilizers and pesticides, and by education of farmers.

The Green Revolution has not succeeded, because it depended on a high level of expensive technology. Most irrigation schemes required capital investment beyond the nations' means and farmers could not afford the fertilizers necessary to produce the high yields from the new crop strains. Countries could not afford to import the machinery, spare parts, petroleum, and fertilizers required. One result was that they became even more indebted to the developed nations. Failure in many areas occurred, because farmers did not understand how to apply the modern methods.

4 Land reform

In many areas of the world, farming plots are too small. Also, they are often divided into tiny strips, scattered over a wide area. This is called **fragmentation**. The plots become smaller and more fragmented with the sharing of land between successive generations. The improvement of farming techniques is impossible under such circumstances. Many farmers do not own their land, but rent it from absentee landlords, often for a proportion of the harvest. This is called **share-cropping**, and it has two bad effects: it makes farmers reluctant to improve the land, and it prevents them earning money by selling crops.

Land reform can be a solution. Consolidation of holdings means grouping plots together and making them larger. To do this, all the local farmers must agree, and alternative employment must be provided for some of them. In some countries, land has been redistributed, so that farmers own the land they cultivate, and land tenure has been made more secure.

5 Intermediate technology

Advanced technology is not always suited to the farming patterns of developing countries. However, improvements can be made by introducing **intermediate technology**. This involves the use of simple technology to improve methods of cultivation, e.g. a better design of ox-drawn plough. Water supplies and irrigation are increased by using small-scale methods, e.g. well-digging in India. Barrages are constructed by manual labour in water catchment areas to provide small reservoirs. In Botswana, iron tanks are sunk into the ground and rainfall is made to collect in the tanks.

Expanding the resource base – examples

1 Reclamation of the Zuyder Zee, Netherlands

Work began in 1920 on a plan to add to the cultivated area of the Netherlands and reduce flood risks. A 29 km. dyke was built from the coast of North Holland to the Friesland coast, converting the inland sea of the Zuyder Zee into Lake IJssel (IJsselmeer). After this, the reclamation of IJsselmeer was begun. Wieringermeer, 20 000 hectares in size, was the first polder to be drained. This was followed in 1942 by the draining of the north-east polder, then East and South Flevoland (fig. 4).

To reclaim polders, a ring dyke was constructed around the area, then drainage channels were made by floating dredgers, and the water pumped out. After a few years, when the ground was firm, cultivation could begin. Finally other elements of the landscape were added: roads, bridges, farms, villages, etc.

The reclamation of the Zuyder Zee has been very important to the Netherlands, because it has improved the safety of the country. Water from Lake IJssel provides water supplies for the farms, and the barrier dam has provided a route for a motorway linking Holland

Fig. 4 Reclamation of the Zuyder Zee.

and the north-east. The first two polders were mainly used for agriculture. Arable farming has been diversified into livestock and mixed farming, and also horticulture. Urbanization has been so rapid that the two Flevo polders are taking overspill from the Randstad. Close to Amsterdam, the city of Aalsmeer is being constructed. Land for recreation has also been made available.

2 Oil exploitation in Abu Dhabi

Oil was discovered in Abu Dhabi, a tiny sheikdom on the Persian Gulf, in 1958. Abu Dhabi's income multiplied as the price of crude oil soared. Abu Dhabi has become one of the richest countries in the world, measured by income per head of population. Signs of this are evident in the massive developments of buildings, offices and roads. However, oil is the only export, and so the government is planning for the time when oil runs out by investing some of the revenue in projects of diversification.

Oil-based industries are being introduced, including a petrochemical complex to produce PVC and soda, chemical plants to produce chlorine, ozone and sulphuric acid, and a cement plant.

There are plans for expanding the fishing industry and for developing attractions for tourists. Agriculture has not been forgotten. Water is provided from desalination plants that process sea water. Vegetables are grown in the winter, while in the summer, when temperatures reach over 38°C, too high for growth, production comes from refrigerated greenhouses.

K ▶ Development and aid

Development is assisted by aid programmes. Most developed countries supply aid. A small percentage of each nation's income is devoted to developing countries. There have been calls for much greater financial commitment from prosperous countries, and for reductions in interest rates on loans.

Some prestige aid programmes have been carried out. Russia helped to finance the Aswan Dam scheme and China helped to build the Tanzam railway across Tanzania and Zambia. However, most valuable aid is given by the United Nations and through the work of voluntary organizations. National financial aid is given to governments of developing countries, but it is only effective if used responsibly, e.g. invested in agricultural improvements rather than in defence.

Much of the effective aid for improvement of land, farming techniques, irrigation, health and education comes from voluntary organizations. These are charitable bodies which raise money to finance projects. Instead of working through governments, they send out their own teams to research and oversee the projects. These organizations include the Red Cross, Oxfam, Christian Aid and Cafod. However they face two major problems. One is the uncertainty of their funds and the need for fund-raising. The other is the high frequency of natural disasters and wars. Much of their relief work is short term, helping victims of drought, floods, disease, earthquakes, wars, etc. It diverts funds from long-term relief operations, which in many ways are the most important. This is because they are designed to help people become self-sufficient so that they will no longer need aid.

K ▶ Trade

The resources of the world are distributed unevenly. As a result, trade has developed between regions and nations. The main commodities moved are raw materials, particularly oil and iron ore, foodstuffs, and finished products. The exports of a country provide the income with which it can purchase its imports. The balance between exporting and importing is known as the **balance of**

payments. A surplus occurs when the income earned from exports is greater than the cost of imports. There is a deficit when the imports cost more than the income from exports. Visible exports and imports are goods. Invisible exports or imports are activities that earn or cost foreign currency, like services and tourism. A number of European countries have a negative balance of payments for products, but the deficit is covered by invisible exports.

Most developing countries have a negative balance of payments, because most of their exports, although great in bulk, are low in value, e.g. foodstuffs and raw materials. Their main imports are small in bulk, except for oil, but of high value: machinery, finished goods, pharmaceuticals. In order to improve their balance of payments, developing countries need to export more manufactured goods and reduce their dependence on imported technology.

Trading patterns do not help to solve these problems. Some developed countries have tariffs, and they have the power to keep commodity prices low because there is no alternative market for the developing countries to export to. Industries in the developed world are dependent on cheap raw materials and wages that reflect low food prices.

The two main trading bodies of the world are the USA and the EEC. The EEC has 19 per cent of world trade, importing about 50 per cent of its energy needs and 75 per cent of its raw materials. The USA has 14 per cent of world trade.

Summary

1 Development is measured by the gross national product (GNP). Birth rates, life expectancy, level of literacy, calorie consumption and numbers employed in agriculture are also indicators of development.

2 Insufficient food production is the result of poor farming techniques, insufficient productive land, natural disasters and rapid population increase.

3 Food production can be increased by irrigation, soil management, the use of technology and land reform.

4 Development can be helped through aid from charities or governments

5 The balance of payments is the balance between the exports and imports of a country. Many developed countries have a surplus, while most developing countries have a deficit.

Questions

1 (a) Name two countries with a high GNP, and two countries with a low GNP.

(b) From fig. 3, name two countries with a high calorie consumption and two countries with a low calorie consumption.

(c) Give two other ways of measuring the level of development of a country and explain why each is considered to be a useful indicator of development.

2 (a) Name two charities which help developing countries.

(b) What is meant by 'temporary relief'?

(c) Describe the advantages to the developed countries of sending government aid, rather than sending aid through a charity.

(d) Describe two problems that have occurred in developing countries by the misuse of aid.

3 Name one region where the resource base is being expanded. How can this help to increase food supplies?

It is not possible to provide full answers to all the questions, because a number of them involve an example of your choice. For those answers, a guide will be given to the kind of information that should be included.

Chapter 1 Diagrams and maps

1 (a) 1960 (b) 1500 million.
2 (a) Yorks., Notts. and Derby. (b) South Wales.
3 (a) USSR. (b) 1.36 million tonnes.
4 (a) Floods. (b) 75 per cent.
5 (a) Brazil. (b) Nearly 50 per cent.
6 (a) 52 per cent. (b) USA.
7 (a) North. (b) SE England.
8 (a) Paris. (b) Italy.
9 (a) Over 16°C. (b) NE Scotland.
10 (a) Under 625 mm. (b) In the west.
11 (a) 121 000. (b) Ireland.
12 (a) Mountaineering, walking, water sports.
(b) Mountains, lakes, coast.
13 (a) Power production, manufacturing, farming, forestry, tourism.
(b) Refer to position relative to river, type of land, proximity to other activities, e.g. factories along river banks on flood plain, close to source of power.
14 (a) Orchards and arable, woodland, vineyards.
(b) Old hard rocks.

Chapter 2 Ordnance Survey maps

1 (a) Church with spire. (b) Electricity pylon.
2 177504. **3** SE (SSE). **4** 1.44 km.
5 Fort (dismantled); trackway; Chapel (remains of); Fredley Manor.
6 (a) Absence of surface drainage; dry valley; escarpment.
(b) National Trust land, footpaths and bridleways.
7 Mickleham: mainly linear, church at centre. Westhumble: rectilinear, large, mainly off main road.

8 Cross-section 160513 to 175513: left-hand side, gentle slope down to river, then fairly level area of flood plain, with steep slope upwards, scarp slope on right-hand side.

9 (a) Sketch map: valley region occurs on the left half of sketch map, downs on the right. The railway line and the A roads, mainly north-south, should be drawn through the valley region.
(b) Main communications along the valley where land is level and along the base of the scarp slope, but very few roads and no railway in the higher and steeper area.

Chapter 3 The nature of the earth

1 (a) Should be similar to fig. 14, page 21, but not in three dimensions. The blocks are each side of the valley, the faults are at the boundary of the valley and the fault scarps are the steep slopes bordering the valley.

2 (a) Granite, e.g. Dartmoor: rounded hills, tors, wide river valleys, poor drainage, moorland.
(b) Uplands: poor soils, poor farming.

3 (a) Syncline.
(b) The level to which pervious rock is saturated with groundwater.

Chapter 4 Shaping the landscape

1 (a) Differences: upper valley is V-shaped, with interlocking spurs; intermediate valley has meanders and flood plains.
(b) In the upper reaches, the river is engaged in vertical erosion, producing a V-shaped valley with interlocking spurs. In the intermediate stage, lateral erosion and deposition are taking place, forming meanders and flood plains.

2 Name of river. Description of urban/industrial development. Explanation: e.g. purity of water destroyed by pollution, erosion checked by artificial channel, flood plain deposition prevented, run-off slowed.

3 Name of river or lake. Sources of pollution, e.g. waste disposal, factories, power stations. Types of pollution, e.g. sewage, toxic waste from chemical plants, lead and mercury from chemical, glassware or paper industries.

4 (a) See fig. 17 of chapter 4. Labelling should include undercutting by waves between low and high-tide levels, overhang weathered away to form cliff face.

(b) Conflicting land uses from among the following: tourism; nature conservancy; power production, e.g. oil, coal, nuclear power stations; industrial plants, e.g. iron and steel, chemicals, oil refining; settlement; farming; dairying/market gardening.

Chapter 5   Understanding weather and climate

1 (a) 1008 mb. (b) (i) A line with semi-circles extending from it. (ii) A line with triangles extending from it. (c) (i) Depression. (ii) Anticyclone. (d) Sequence: increase in cloud cover, change of wind direction, rain, rise in temperature, continuing wet and mild until an increase in wind speed, fall in temperature and heavy rain.

2 (a) A: highest temperatures occur between December and February. (b) 881 mm. (c) 21°C in July, −5°C in February. (d) Equatorial climate: uniformly high temperatures, very high rainfall at all seasons.

3 (a) Tropical: tropical cyclone, drought. Temperate: heavy snow, fog, pollution. (b) By forecasting and monitoring, so that precautions are taken, by investment in irrigation schemes, snow clearing machinery, etc., by laws to reduce pollutants in the atmosphere.

Chapter 6   Population

1 (a) Countries of South-East Asia, North-West Europe. (b) Area too dry to support a large population, e.g. Sahara; too hot and wet, with tropical forest, e.g. Zaïre Basin; too high, with low temperatures and rugged relief, e.g. Atlas Mountains. (c) Low level of development, effects of culture, lack of education, high infant mortality rate.

2 (a) India (b) France (c) Nigeria (d) France. (e) By improving sanitation and water supplies, by raising the standards of nutrition, by providing more medical care, e.g. maternity clinics, hospitals, doctors. (f) Lower life expectancy because of high death rate caused by lack of sanitation, impure water supplies, low level of nutrition, lack of medical care. Higher percentage in lower age groups because of the high birth rate.

3 and 4   Name the region. Reasons for population density include resources available, the type of economy, communications, the level of development, culture and society.

Chapter 7 Where people live

1 (a) Nucleated: around a centre or focus, e.g. church, green, crossroads, spring. Linear: elongated along a road, river or canal.
(b) Name example and describe. Site: land on which settlement is built, e.g. flat, sloping, beside river. Location: where the settlement is in relation to other places, e.g. hills, river basins, coast, towns and cities, major communication lines.
(c) Factors like water supply, crossroads, etc. See pages 80 – 1.

2 Features may include neighbourhood residential units, shops, schools, etc.; pedestrian town centres; good communications to industrial estates; attractively laid out, low density with many parks and green spaces; good recreational facilities.

3 (a) Overcrowding, shanty towns, temporary dwellings, absorbing surrounding settlements, high-rise government and office buildings in contrast to low level of accommodation, traffic congestion, increase in shops and services – description.
(b) Answer depends on choice of city: advantages may include more potential for manufacturing and service industries because of larger market, easier to provide education and improve standards in urban than rural areas. Disadvantages: increased risk of disease, poorer diet, difficulties of administration, too many resources concentrated in one place.

Chapter 8 Farming

1 (a) Market gardening, horticulture, viticulture or rice, e.g. Holland, California, wine-growing region of France or Italy, regions from South-East Asia.
(b) Ranching, e.g. Mid-West, USA; Pampas, Argentina, or Australia.
(c) Monoculture involves the cultivation of only one crop, polyculture involves the cultivation of several crops or crops and livestock.

2 (a) Should look something like fig. 1 of chapter 8, page 94.
(b) Inputs: e.g. seeds, fertilizer, labour, machinery.
Outputs: actual products, by-products.
(c) Physical factors likely to include: rainfall amount and distribution, length of growing season, summer temperatures and sunshine hours, soil type and thickness, the shape, slope and aspect of the land, drainage and water supply.

3 Economic factors likely to include: distance, density and size of settlements, transport, degree of affluence of population, degree of mechanization, marketing and government policy.

Chapter 9 Resources for industry

1 (a) Uranium.
(b) Advantages: small quantities only of fuel required, plants have a high capacity and output, not tied to coalfield or coastal locations. Disadvantages: very high capital cost, need for remote sites, risk of explosions and radioactive leaks.
(c) Level land with a good water supply, remote from major settlements.
(d) Reasons against siting mainly based on danger from radioactivity, e.g. risk of leaks: effects on local population, like cancer, leukaemia, damage to unborn babies, contamination of agricultural land and water supplies. Risk of explosions, e.g. Chernobyl.

2 (a) Name coalfield. Factors may include fall in demand, high cost of extraction, exhaustion of best seams, competition with cheap coal coming from coalfields with lower wages or government subsidies.
(b) Government grants and incentives. Building industrial estates. Improving services and communications. Landscaping, reclaiming and redeveloping derelict land.

3 (a) Primary: produces raw materials. Tertiary: services secondary industry and population (see page 108).
(b) Definition of geographical inertia, see page 111.

Chapter 10 Manufacturing industry

1 (a) Countries located within band shaded with over 50 per cent of exports primary produce. Industrial regions: any of those with solid shading.
(b) For the chosen industrial region: factors aiding development may include presence of raw materials and/or fuel, power supplies, labour, markets, communications.

2 (a) Traditional, e.g. iron and steel, high tech, e.g. computers.
(b) Traditional industries are declining, because of a fall in demand for their products, rationalization of industry, competition from other products, e.g. synthetic materials replacing cotton, wool; plastics replacing steel, competition from industry in the developing world which can produce more cheaply because of lower wage rates.

3 (a) Footloose industries are not tied to specific locational factors (see page 126).
(b) Example, for instance electrical firms, small consumer products.
(c) Describe location with reference to communications, proximity of settlements. Reasons for choice may include those, also nearby residential areas, attractive site, etc.
(d) Modern industrial estate, see page 125.

1 (a) City.
(b) Central location, high-rise blocks, associated with centre of government administration and finance, e.g. Bank of England, Stock Exchange.
(c) May include answers to (b), plus good communications, large labour supply, easy contact between offices.
(d) The high cost of land for building on.

2 (a) May include high cost of travel, transport congestion, high rents and rates, congestion of buildings and lack of room for expansion.
(b) Name the firm and describe its new site and situation. Choice may have been influenced by: environment, cheaper land, communications, lower rents, availability of labour, government grants.

3 (a) Milan: it has the highest index of accessibility.
(b) An integrated pattern of routes.
(c) Italian network: 1.2 Ethiopia: 0.8, according to the index of connectivity (no. of edges ÷ no. of vertices), so Italy has the better connectivity.
(d) Reasons include: door-to-door convenience, rail links are limited, motorways make car journeys easier and quicker, the cost is lower when at least two people are travelling together.

1 (a) Countries with low GNP: selected from the developing world. Countries with high GNP: selected from N America, Europe, Australasia.
(b) Selection made according to areas shaded for under 2000 calories and over 3000 calories.
(c) Level of literacy, birth and death rates, percentage employed in agriculture. As countries become more developed, there is a rise in the level of literacy and falls in the birth rate, death rate and percentage employed in agriculture.

2 (a) e.g. Oxfam, Christian Aid (list on page 150).
(b) Temporary relief is short-term supply for essential needs, like food in a famine. It does not solve any long-term problems, but ensures immediate survival.
(c) Governments have a guaranteed income and much greater resources than voluntary bodies. They can make conditions about the use of aid and can also supply personnel to administer aid, e.g. technicians, agronomists, doctors, etc.

(d) Misuse of aid occurs when aid is redirected into projects that do not bring about a long-term improvement in the situation, and may make the situation worse, e.g. using aid money to buy arms, for bribery and corruption, for prestige undertakings, e.g. new government offices.

3 Name region. With land improvement or reclamation, agricultural production and yields are increased, e.g. Pakistan. With development of other resources, more income is provided to pay for imports of food, e.g. Abu Dhabi.

1 Make sure you have with you the equipment you will need: pen (with spare cartridges or replacement), sharpened lead and coloured pencils, rubber, ruler.

2 Refresh your memory by looking over the list of key words and explanations that you have prepared.

3 Check your OS symbols and your most important maps and diagrams.

4 Work out your time-plan for the examination, e.g. if you have to answer five questions in two hours, allow ten minutes at the beginning to read through the paper, twenty minutes for each question, and the final ten minutes for checking.

5 Make sure that your watch is correct and that you arrive in plenty of time so there is no last-minute rush.

6 Remember to read through the questions slowly and carefully before making your choice. Look in the resource booklet before making your final choice. The questions may not be so easy when you examine the resources you have been given. Do not be put-off if the maps or diagrams relate to an area you have not studied. Check the questions to see if they require specialized knowledge of the area before deciding against that question.

7 Remember, there is no need to panic if your mind goes blank at the beginning of the examination. Relax, read through the questions slowly and start on the easiest. Your memory will soon come back.

8 It is better not to discuss your revision with other students just before the examination. Getting depressed about what you may not have revised is going to put you in the wrong frame of mind to commence the examination.

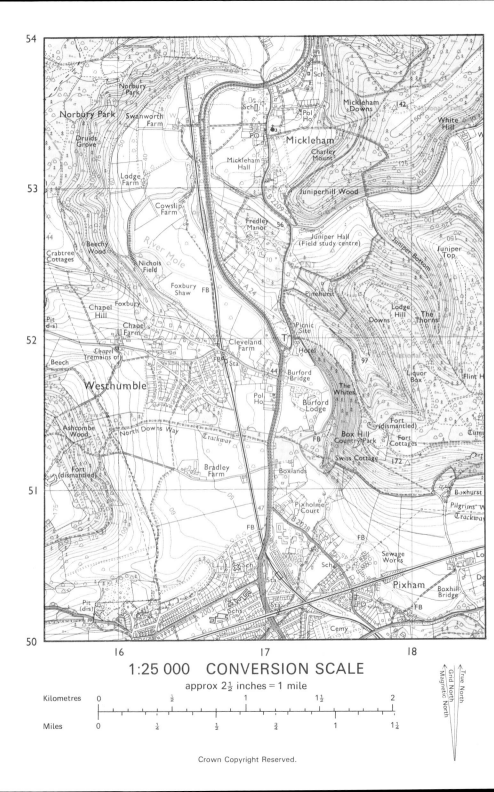

1:25 000 CONVERSION SCALE

approx 2½ inches = 1 mile

Kilometres 0 ——— ½ ——— 1 ——— 1½ ——— 2

Miles 0 ——— ¼ ——— ½ ——— ¾ ——— 1 ——— 1¼

True North
Grid North
Magnetic North